Feathered Critter Friends Vol. IV

Feathered Critter Friends Vol. IV

Rob Benton

Esotericom®

All photographs by Rob Benton

ISBN 978-0-9980682-3-7

All birds depicted herein were photographed in the course of their natural behavior.

No bird was enticed, confined, entrapped, or harassed in any way in the making of these photographs.

Front Cover: Rufous Whistler

Back Cover: Palawan Flowerpecker

7 "But ask the beasts, and they will teach you;
the birds of the air, and they will tell you;

8 or the plants of the earth, and they will teach you;
and the fish of the sea will declare to you.

9 Who among all these does not know that the hand
of the Lord has done this?

10 In His hand is the life of every living thing and the
breath of all mankind."

Job 12: 7-10

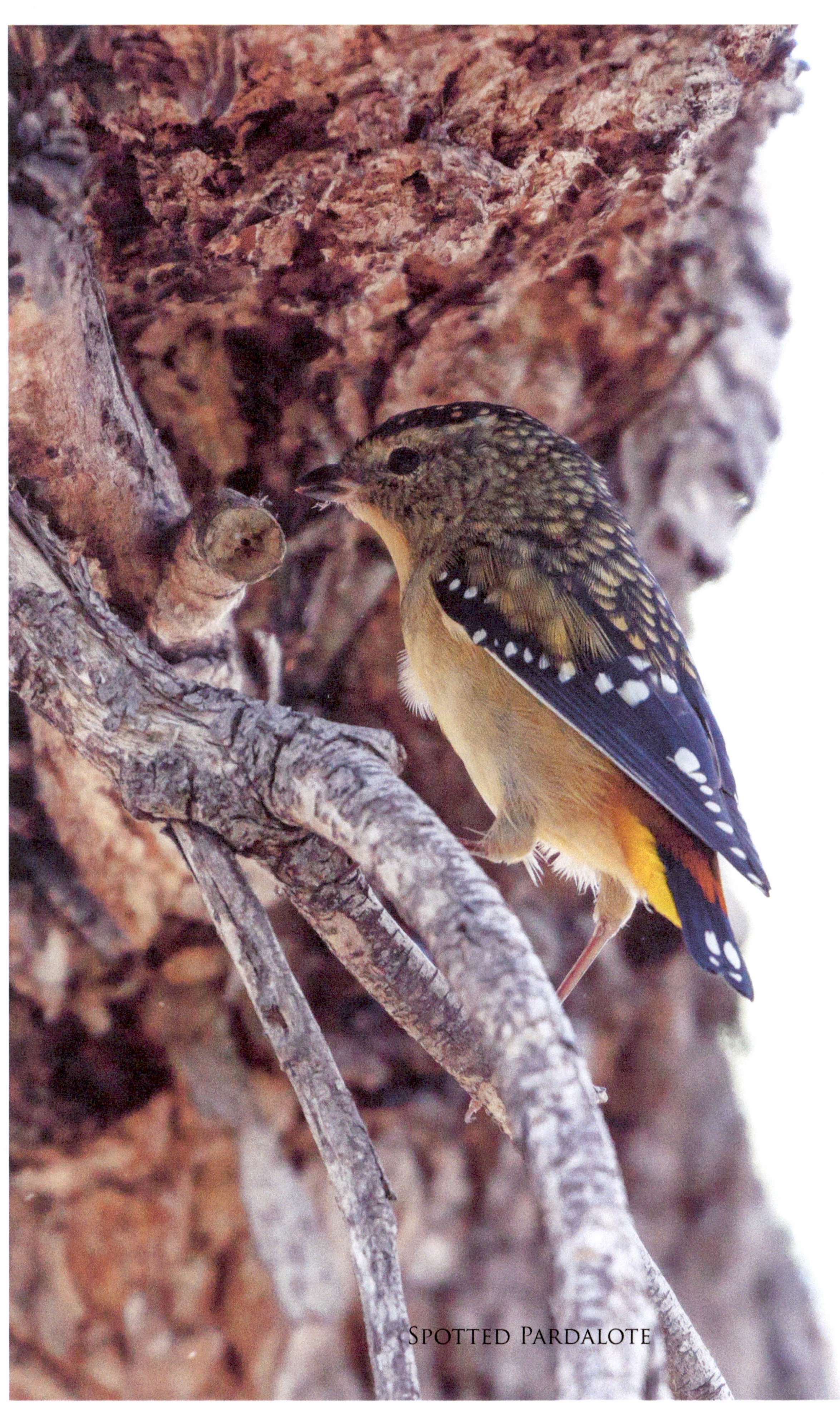

Spotted Pardalote

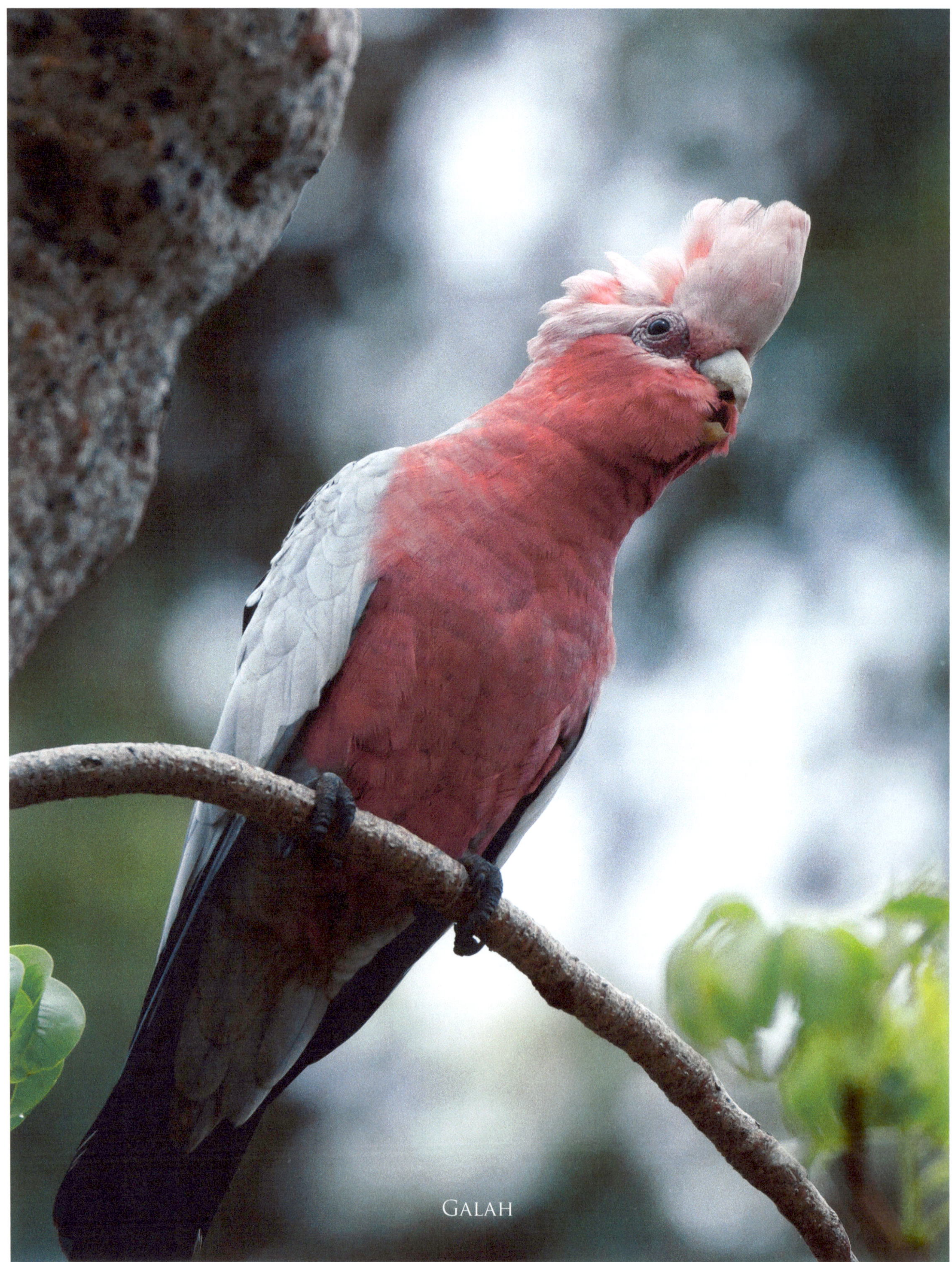

Galah

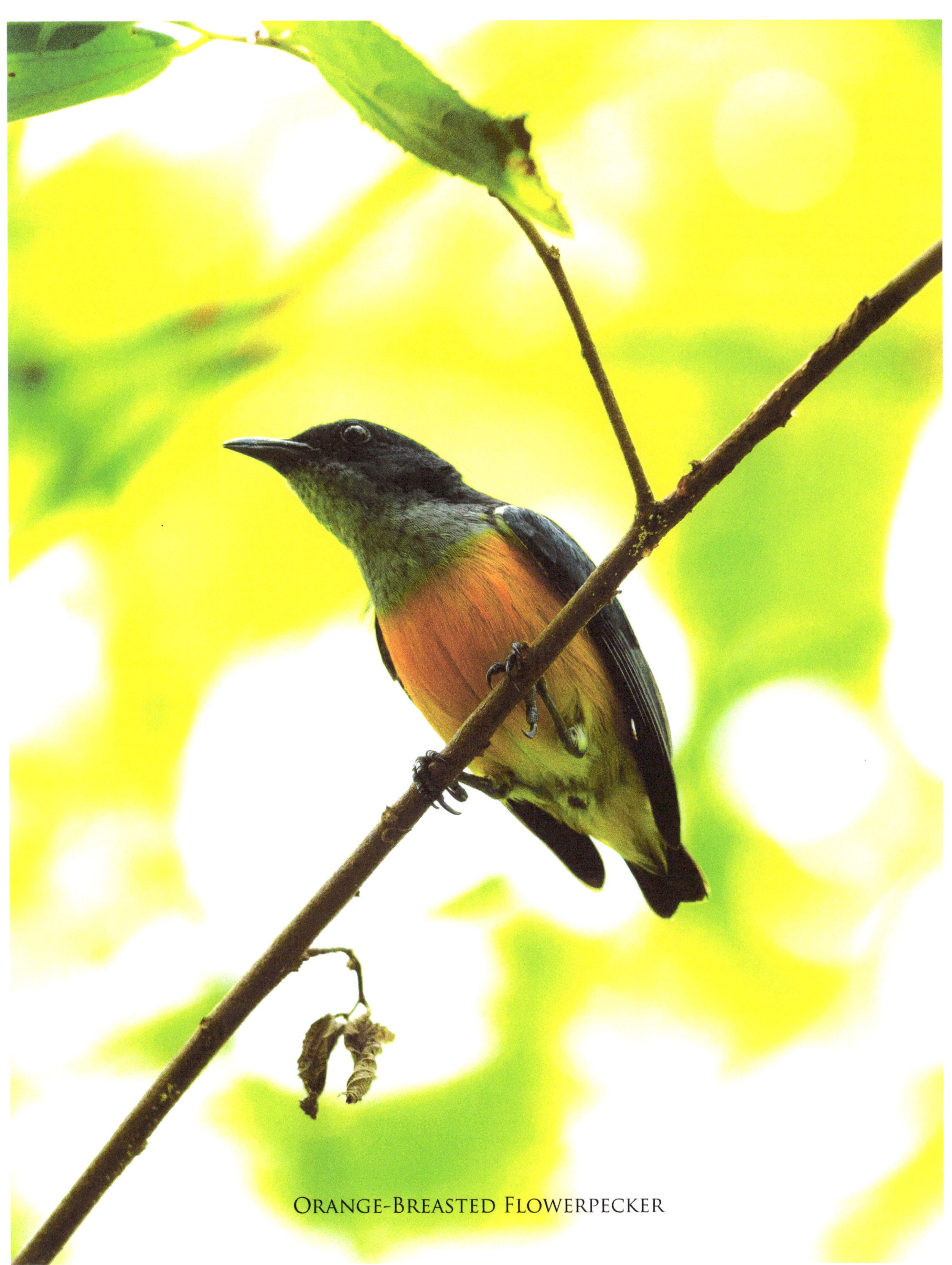

Orange-Breasted Flowerpecker

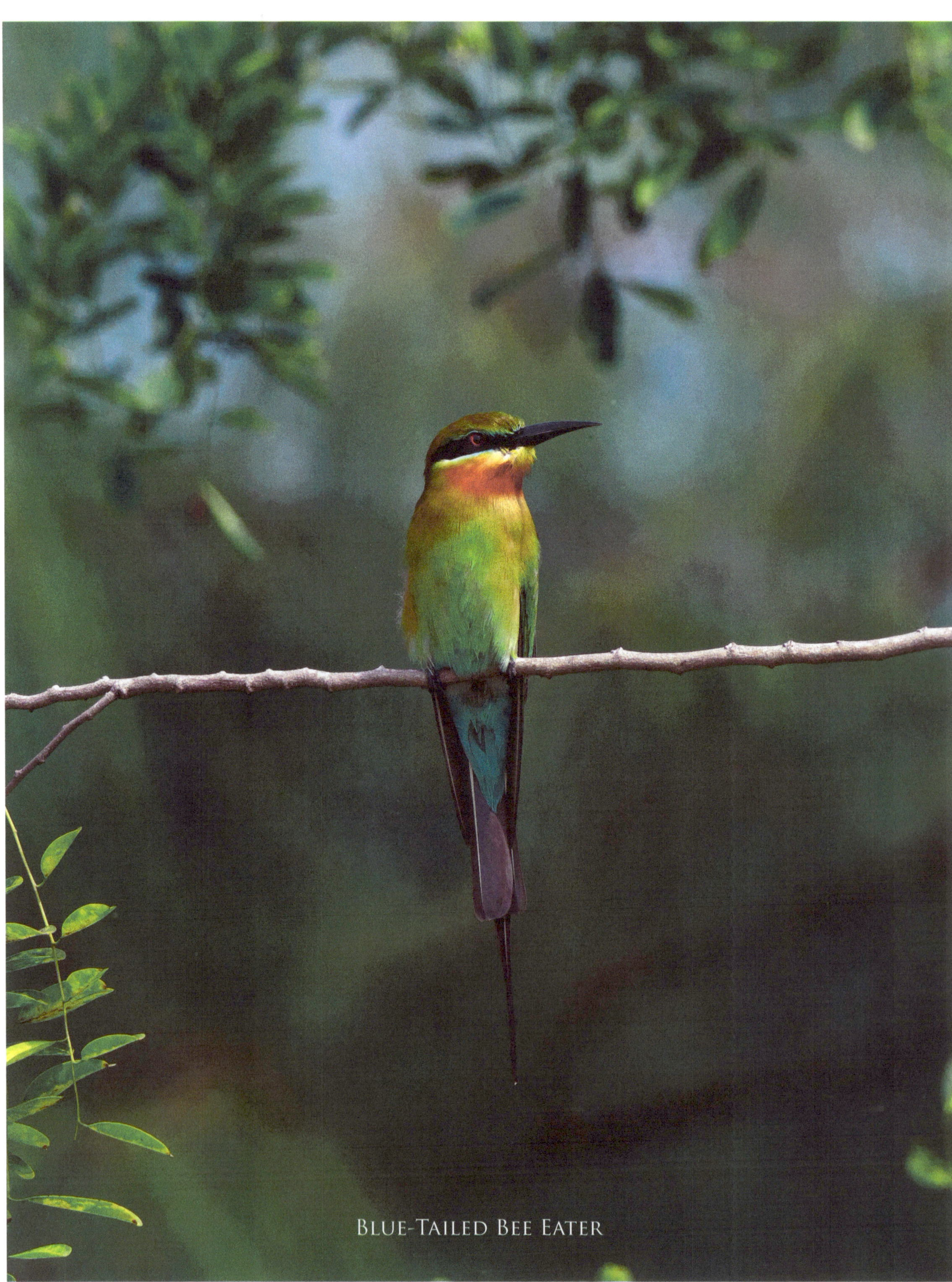

Blue-Tailed Bee Eater

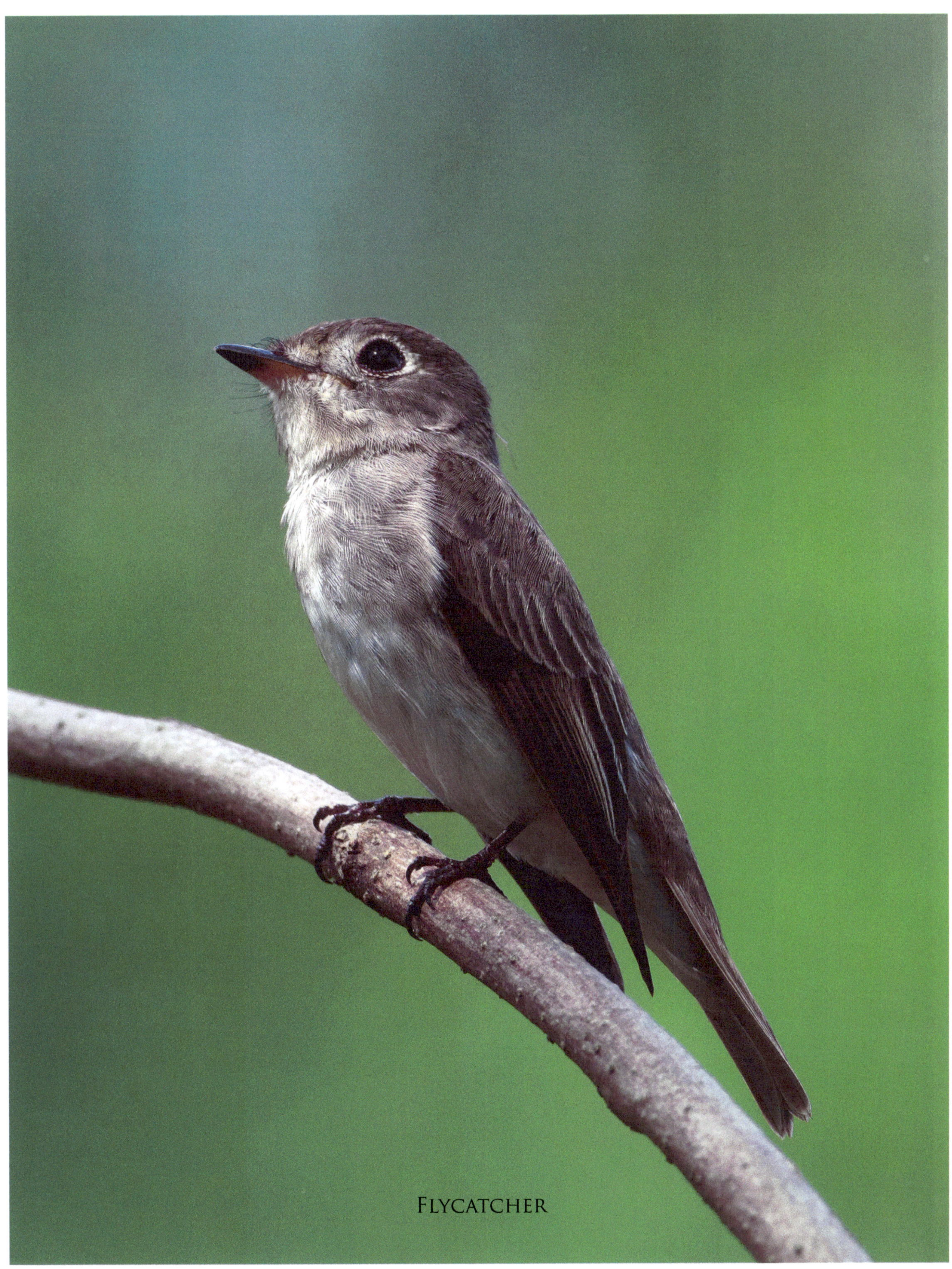

Flycatcher

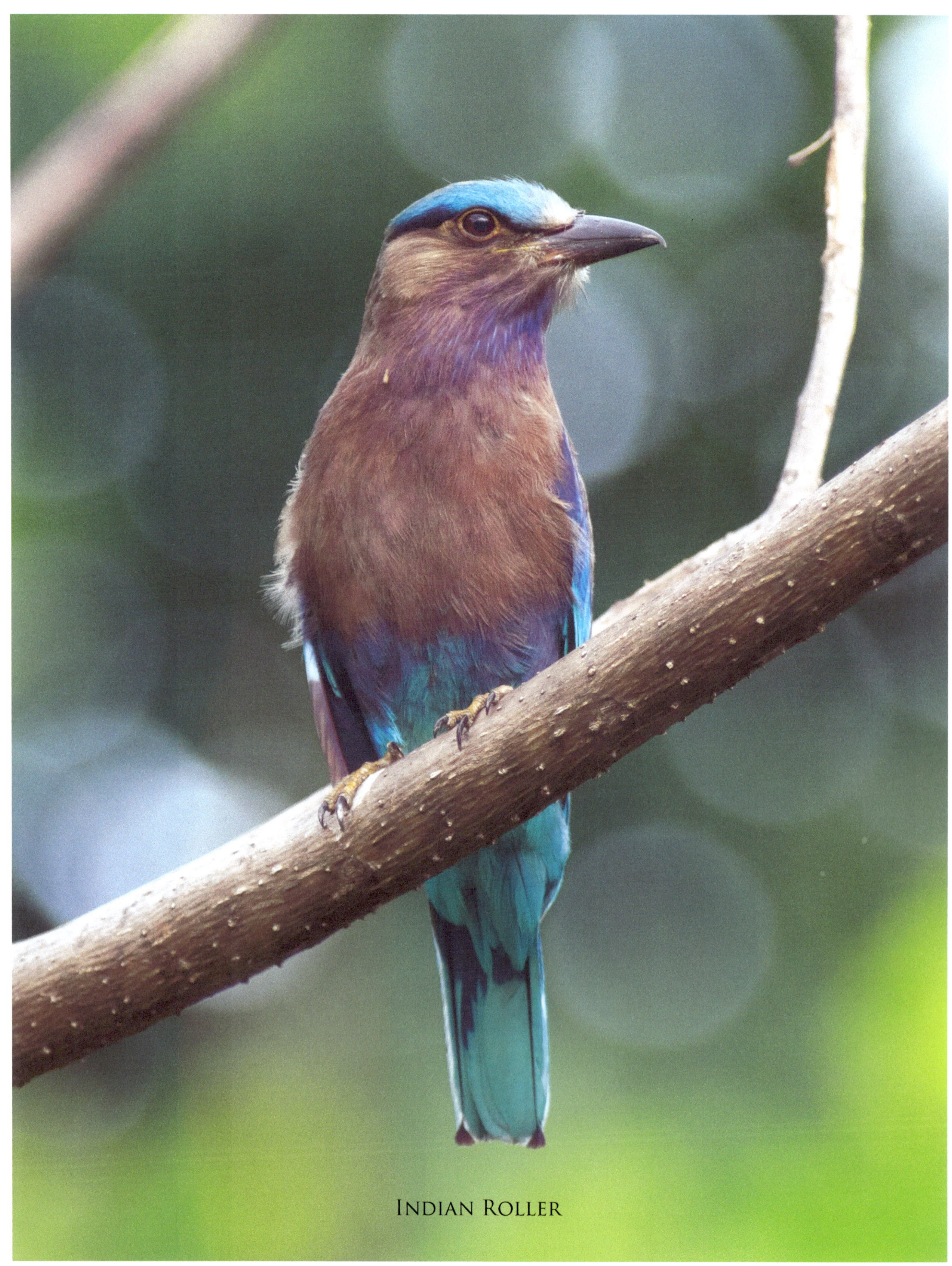

Indian Roller

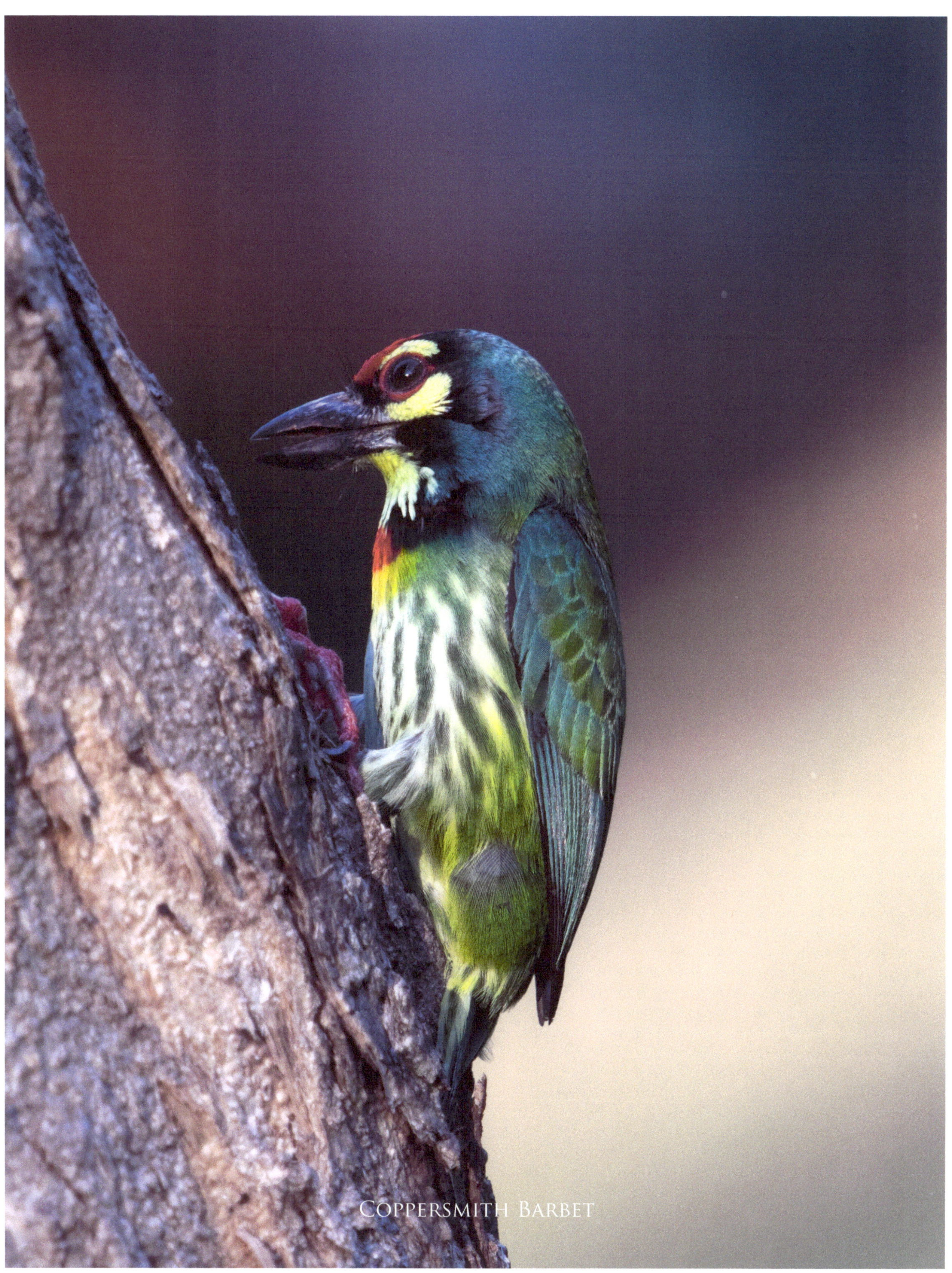

Coppersmith Barbet

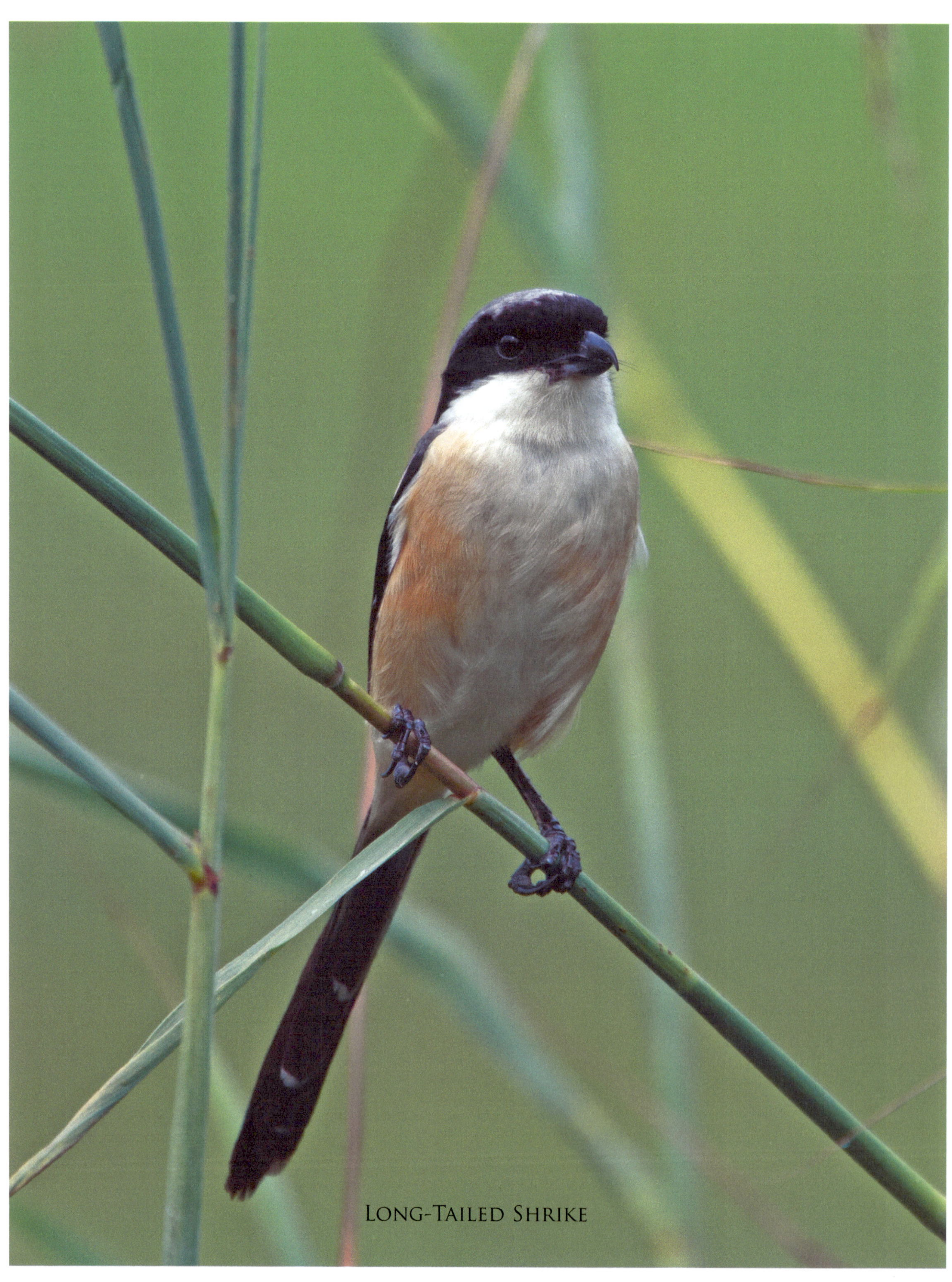

Long-Tailed Shrike

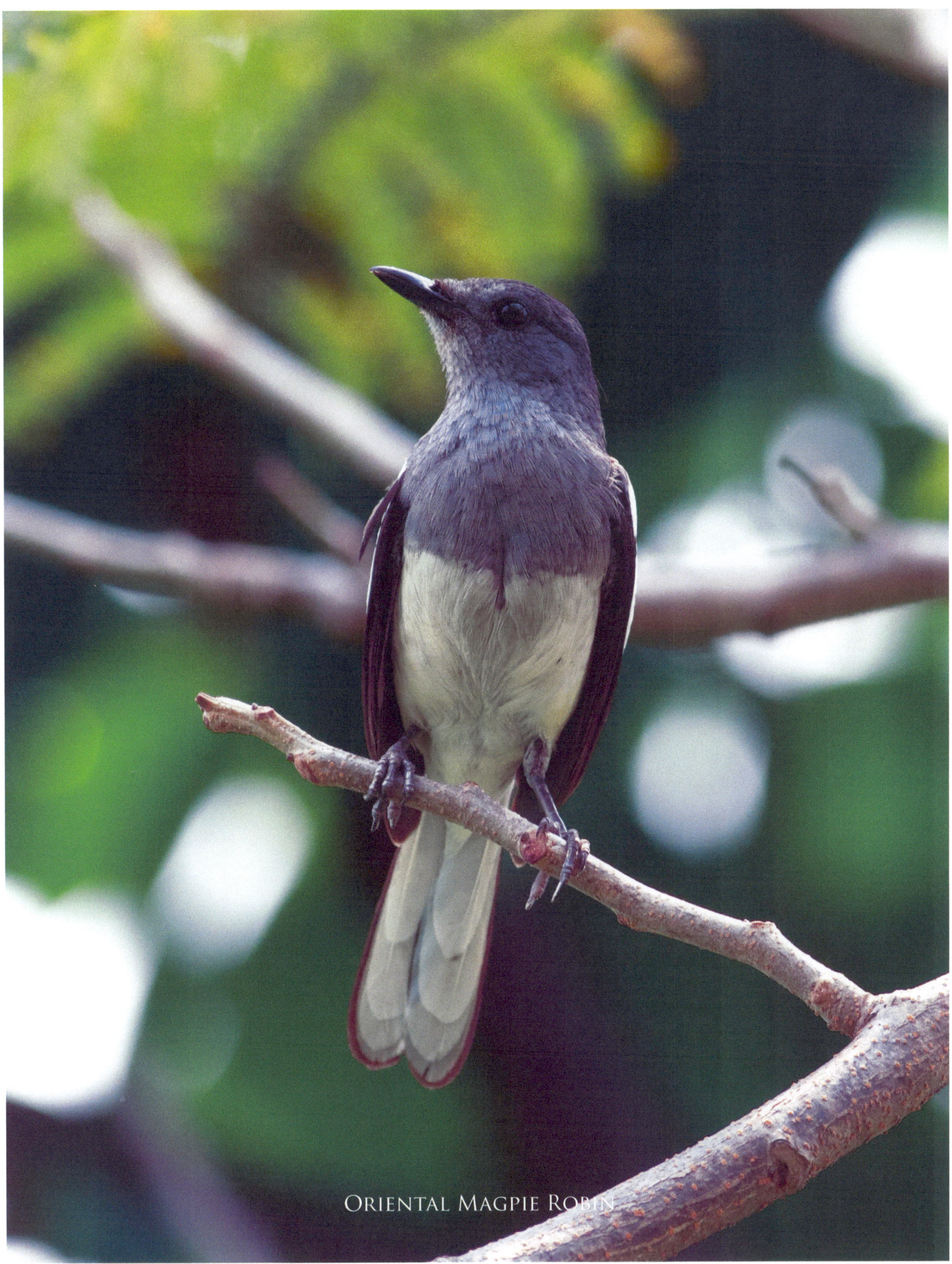

Oriental Magpie Robin

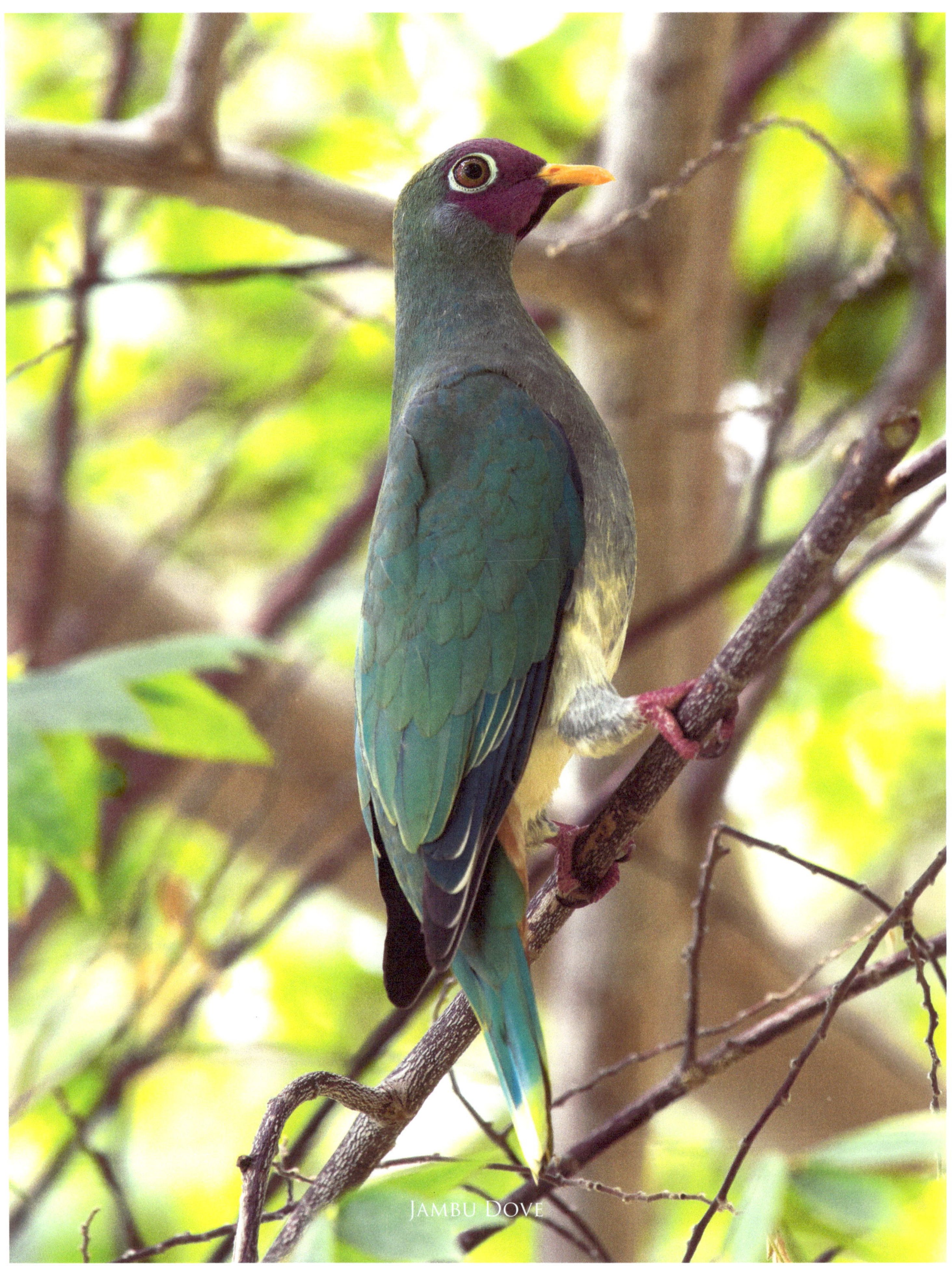

Jambu Dove

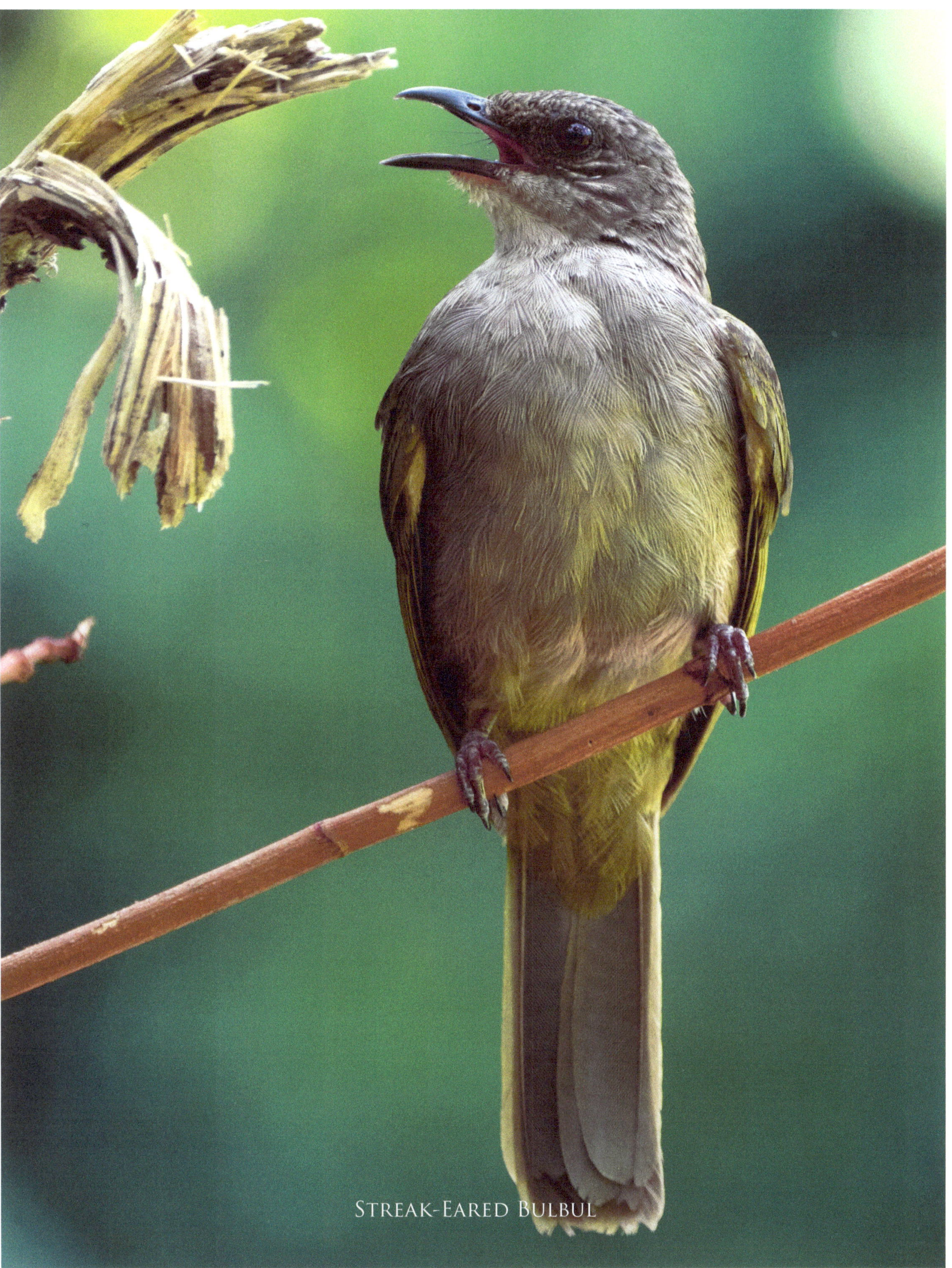

Streak-Eared Bulbul

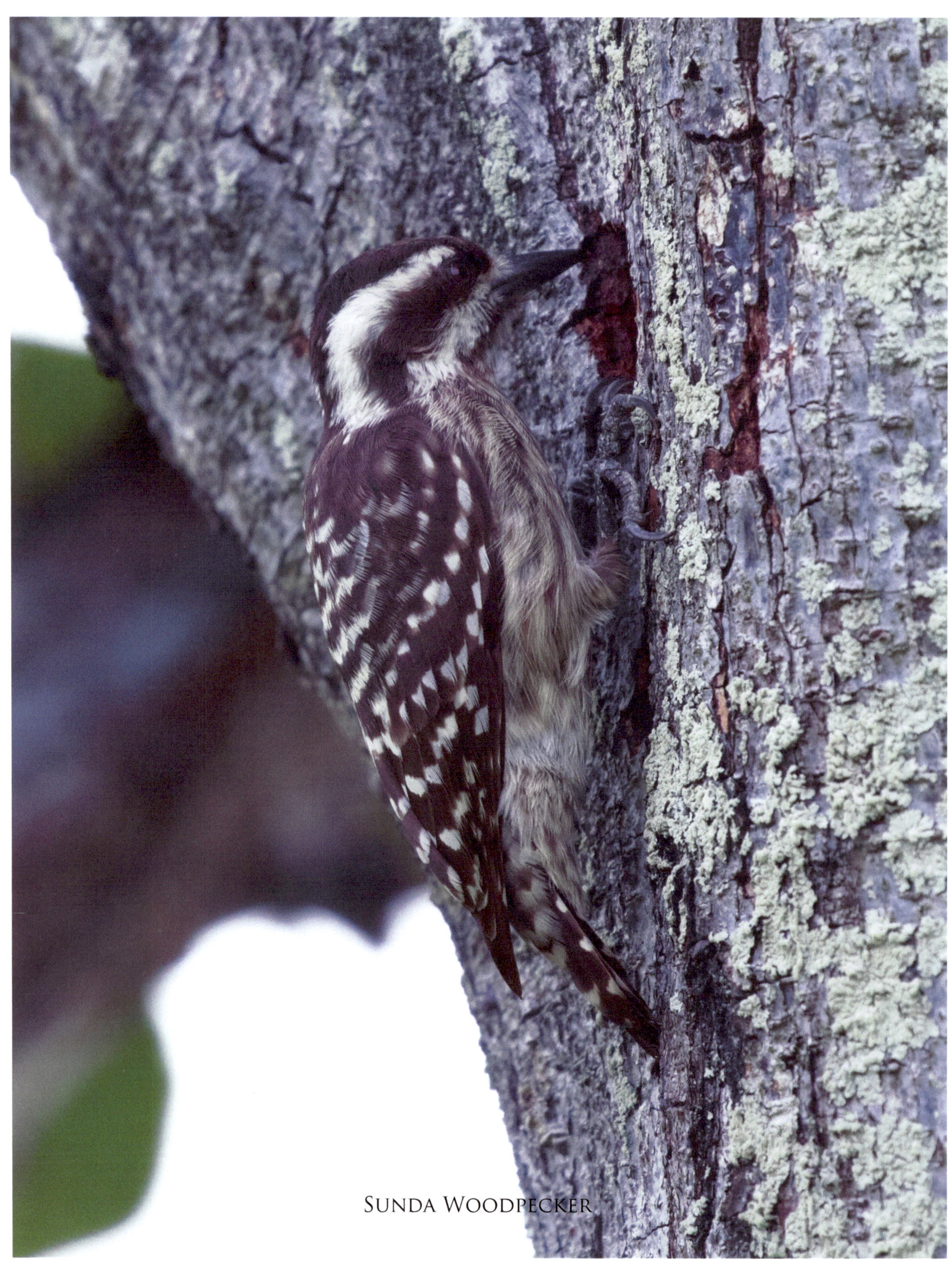

Sunda Woodpecker

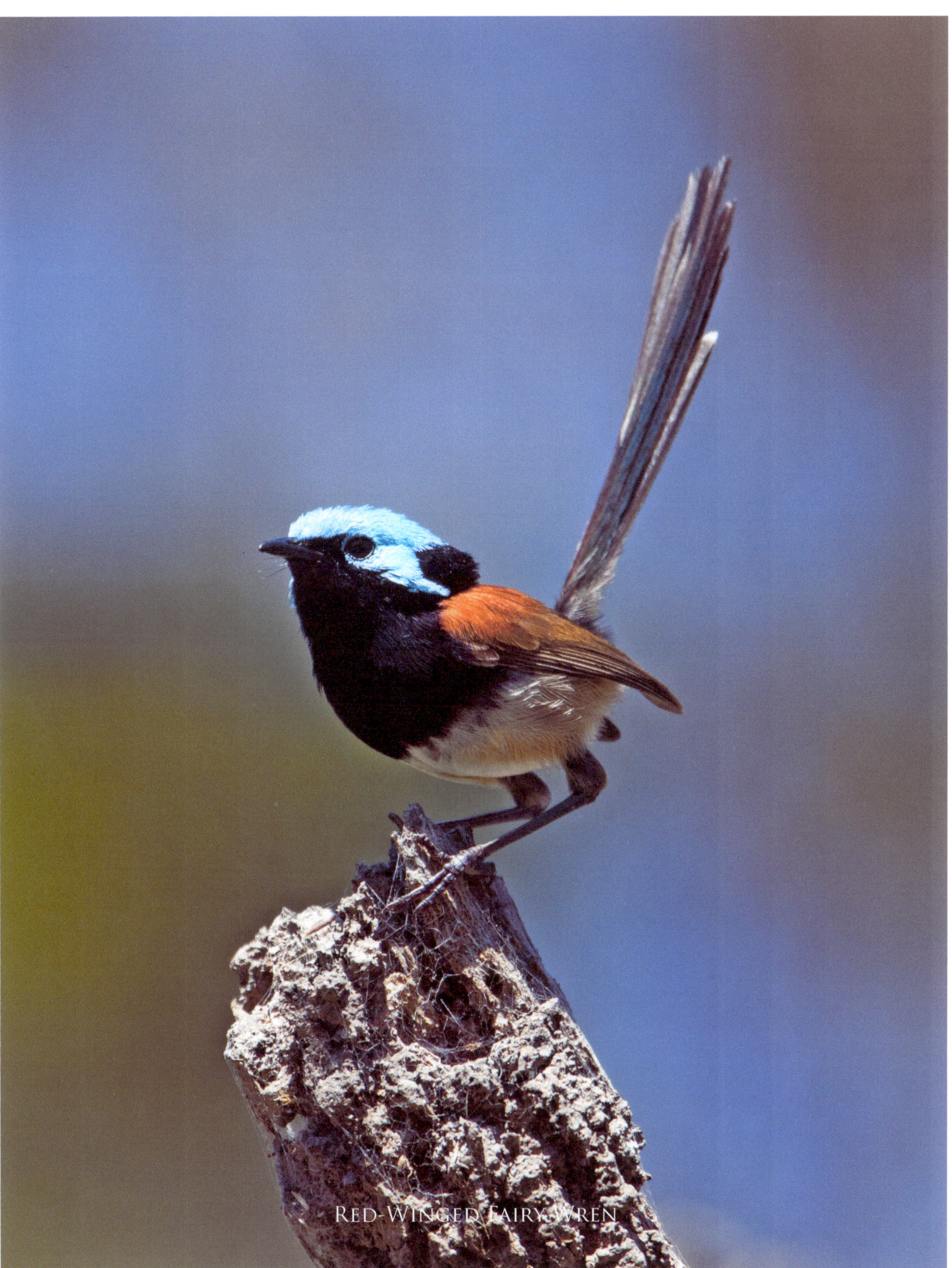

Red-Winged Fairy Wren

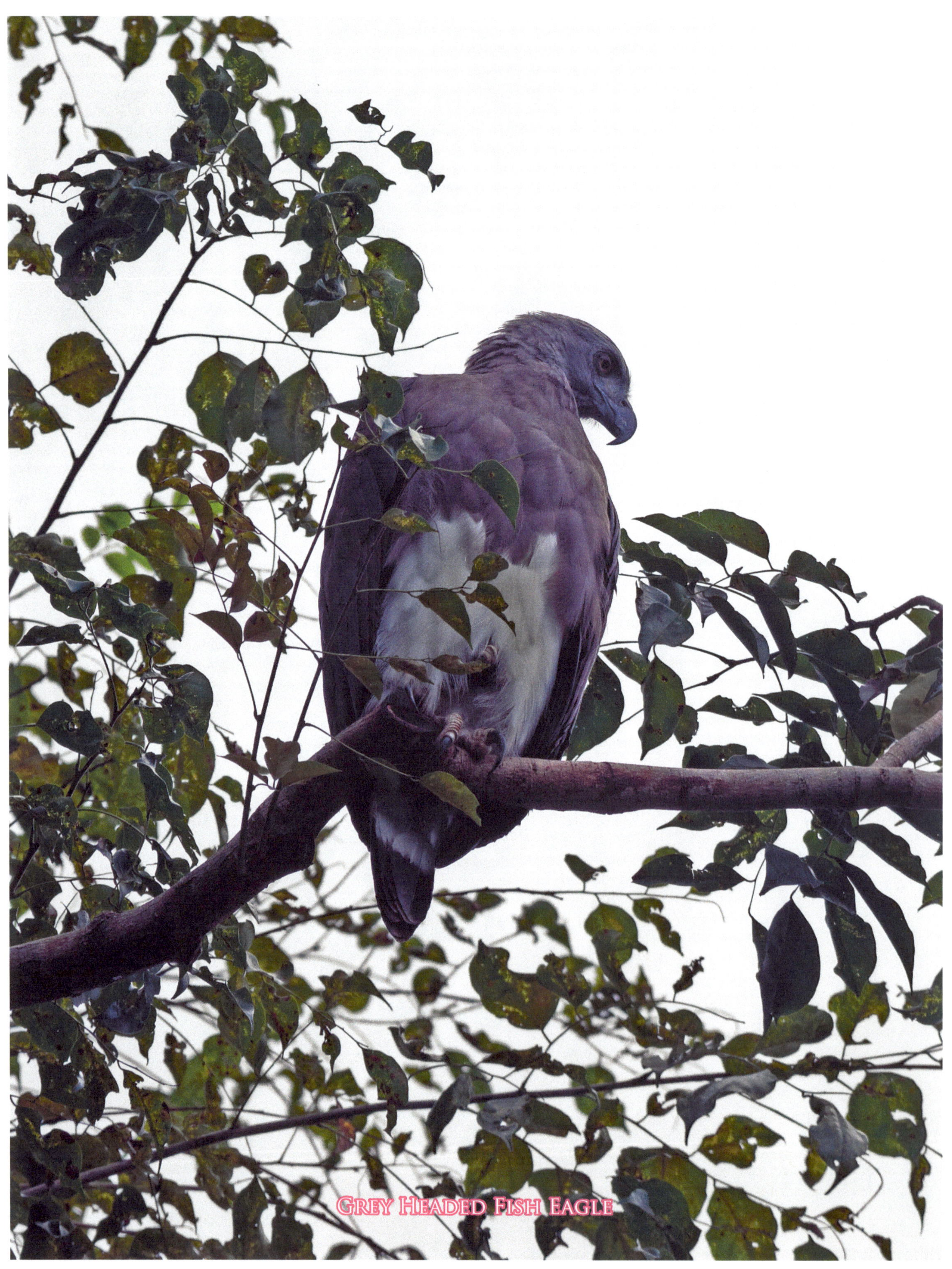

Grey Headed Fish Eagle

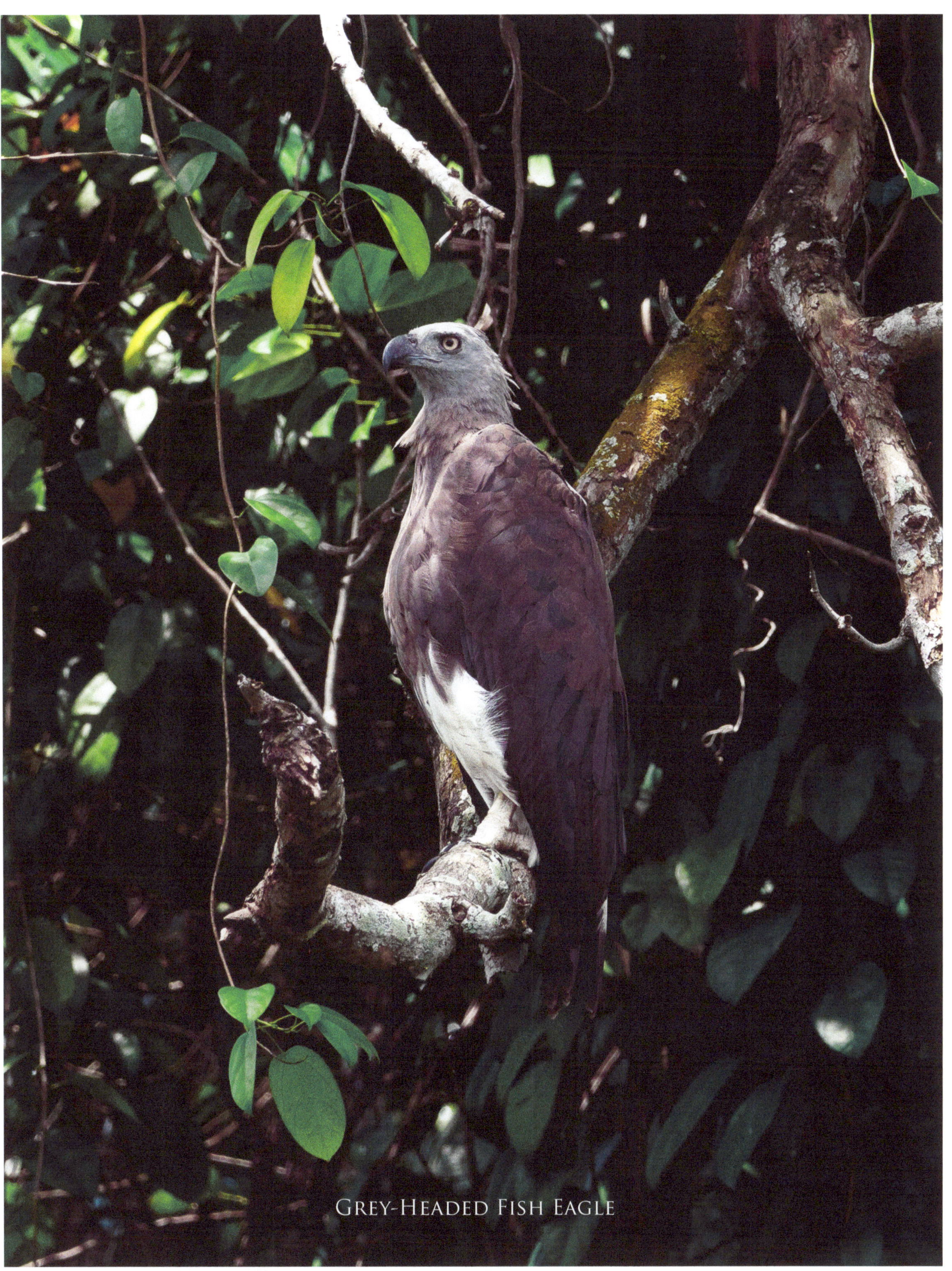
Grey-Headed Fish Eagle

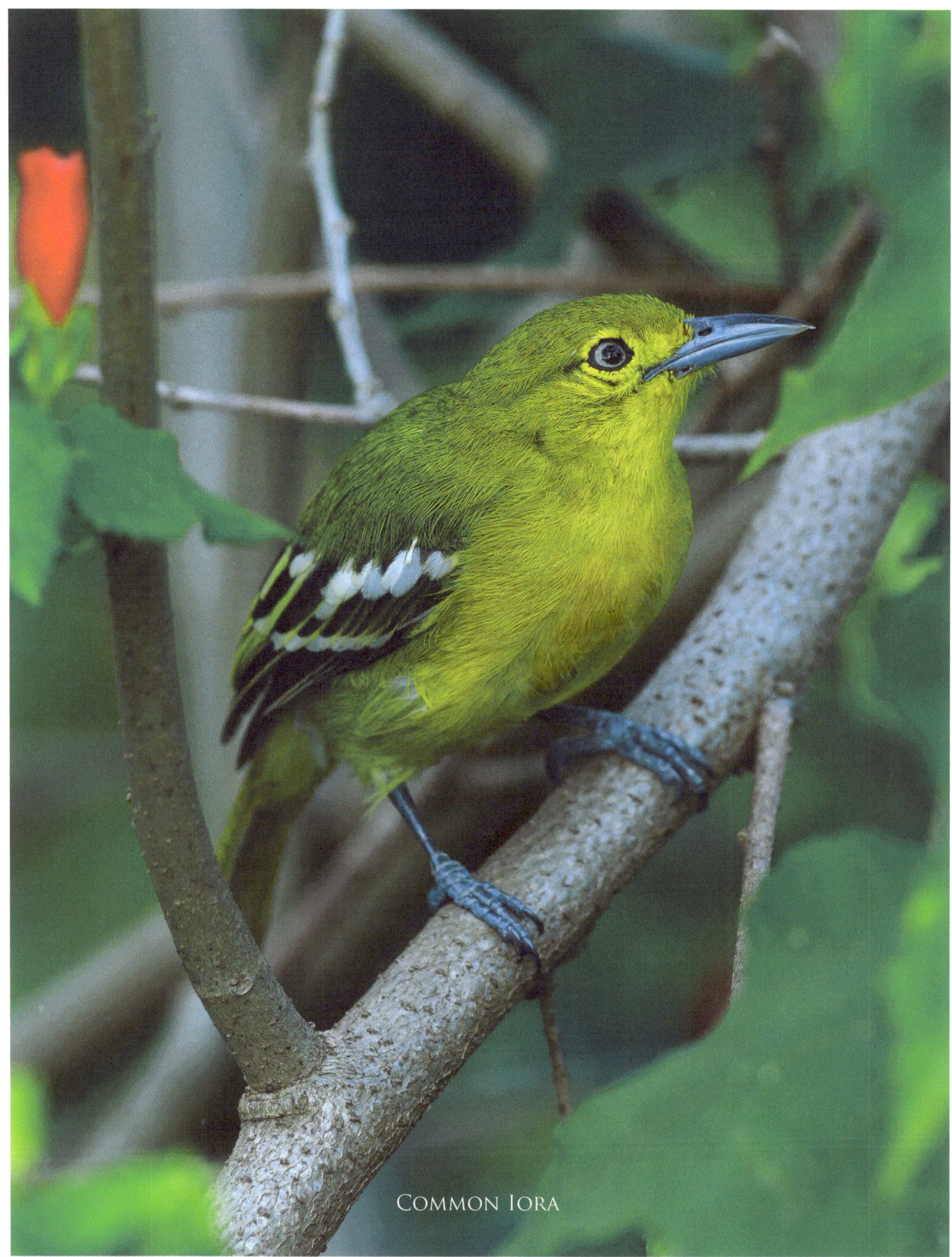
Common Iora

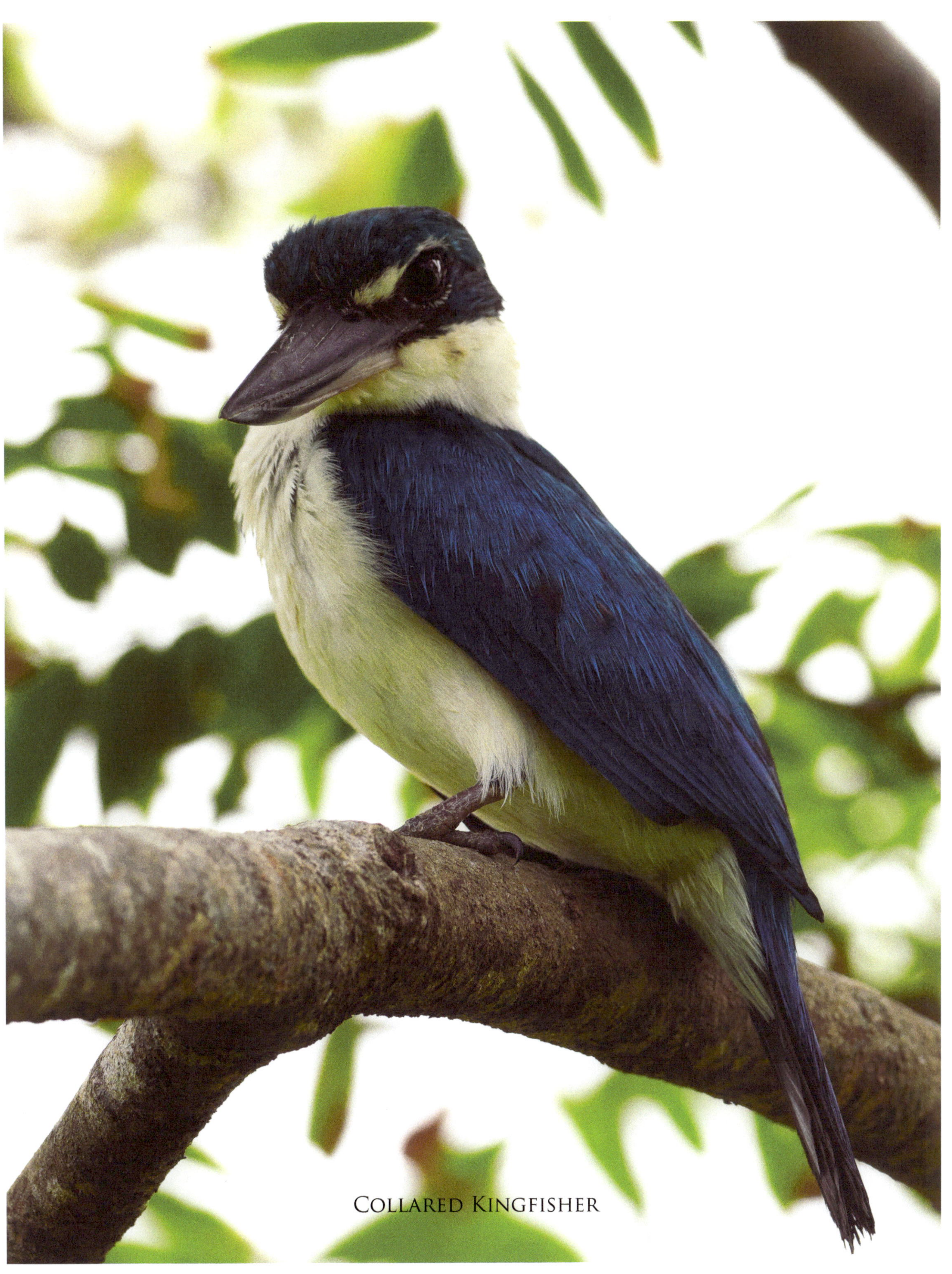
Collared Kingfisher

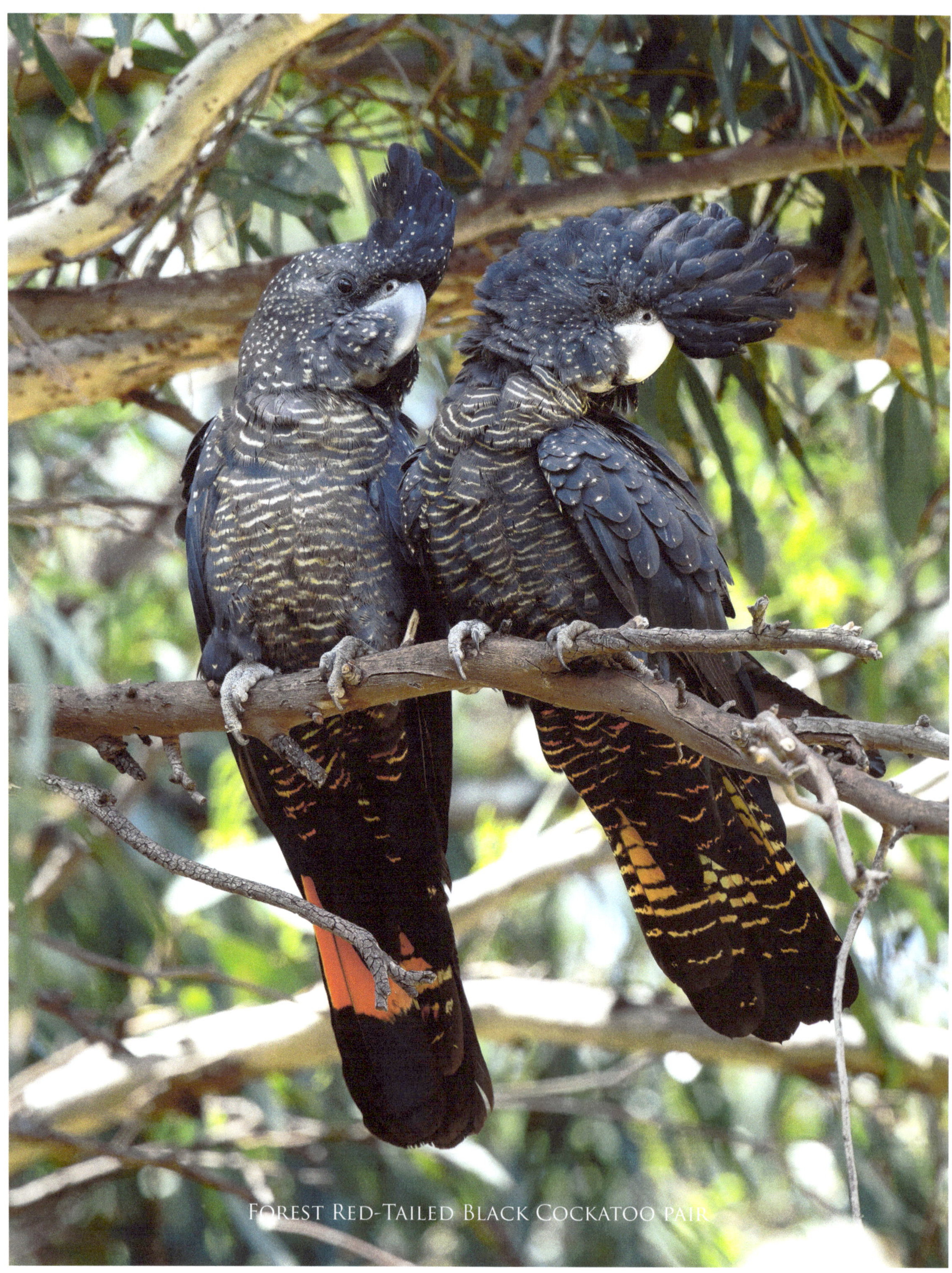

Forest Red-Tailed Black Cockatoo pair

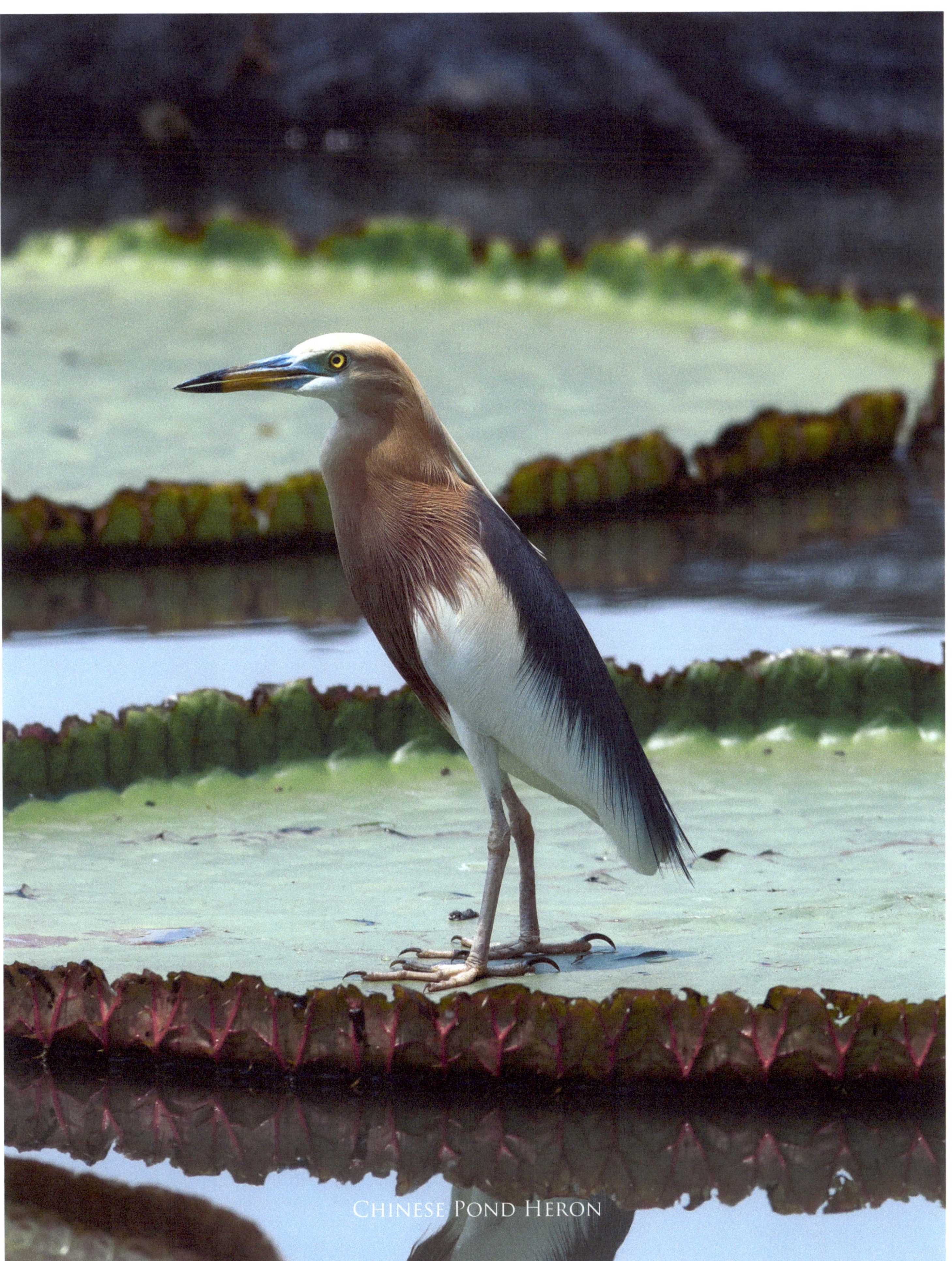
CHINESE POND HERON

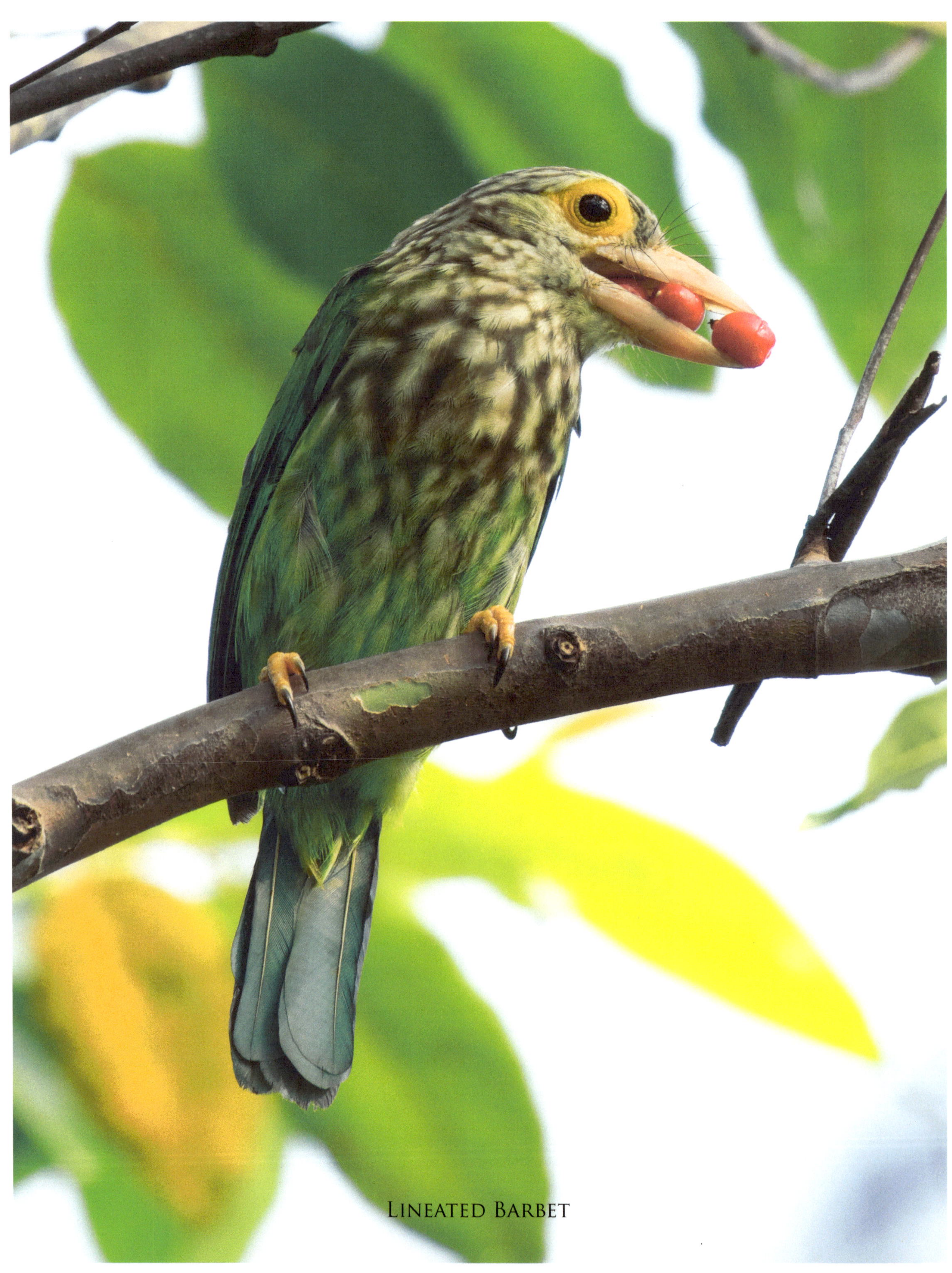

Lineated Barbet

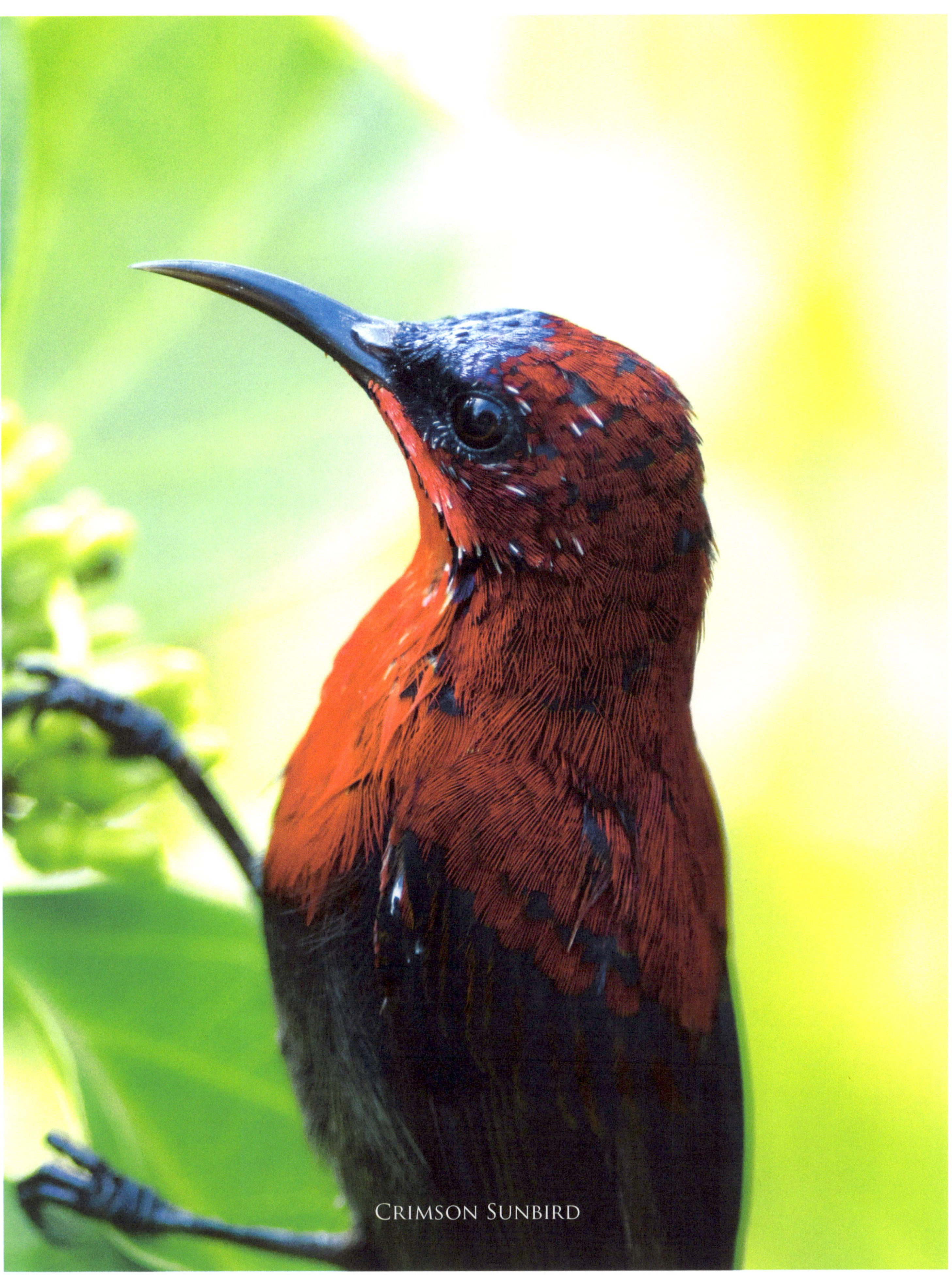

CRIMSON SUNBIRD

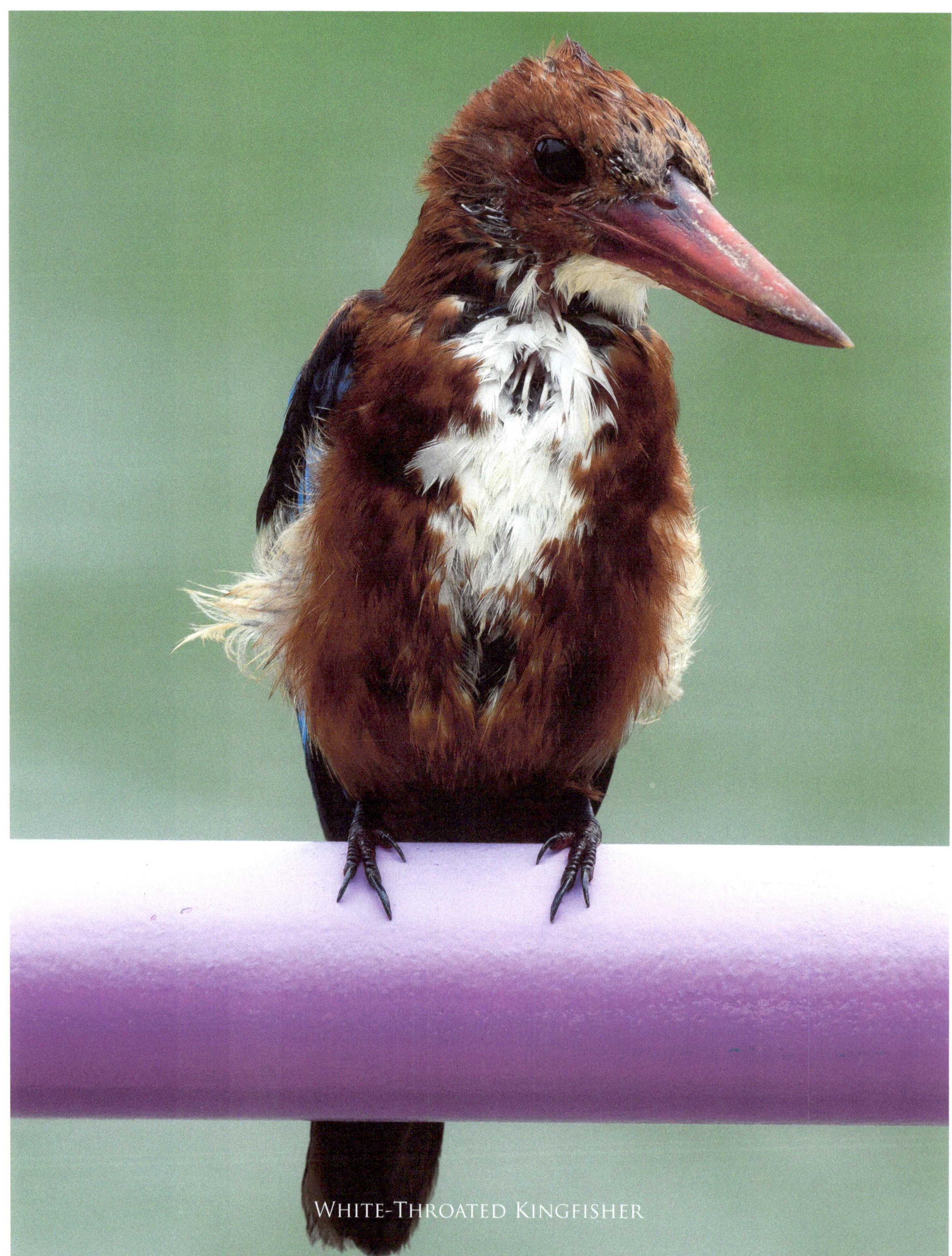
WHITE-THROATED KINGFISHER

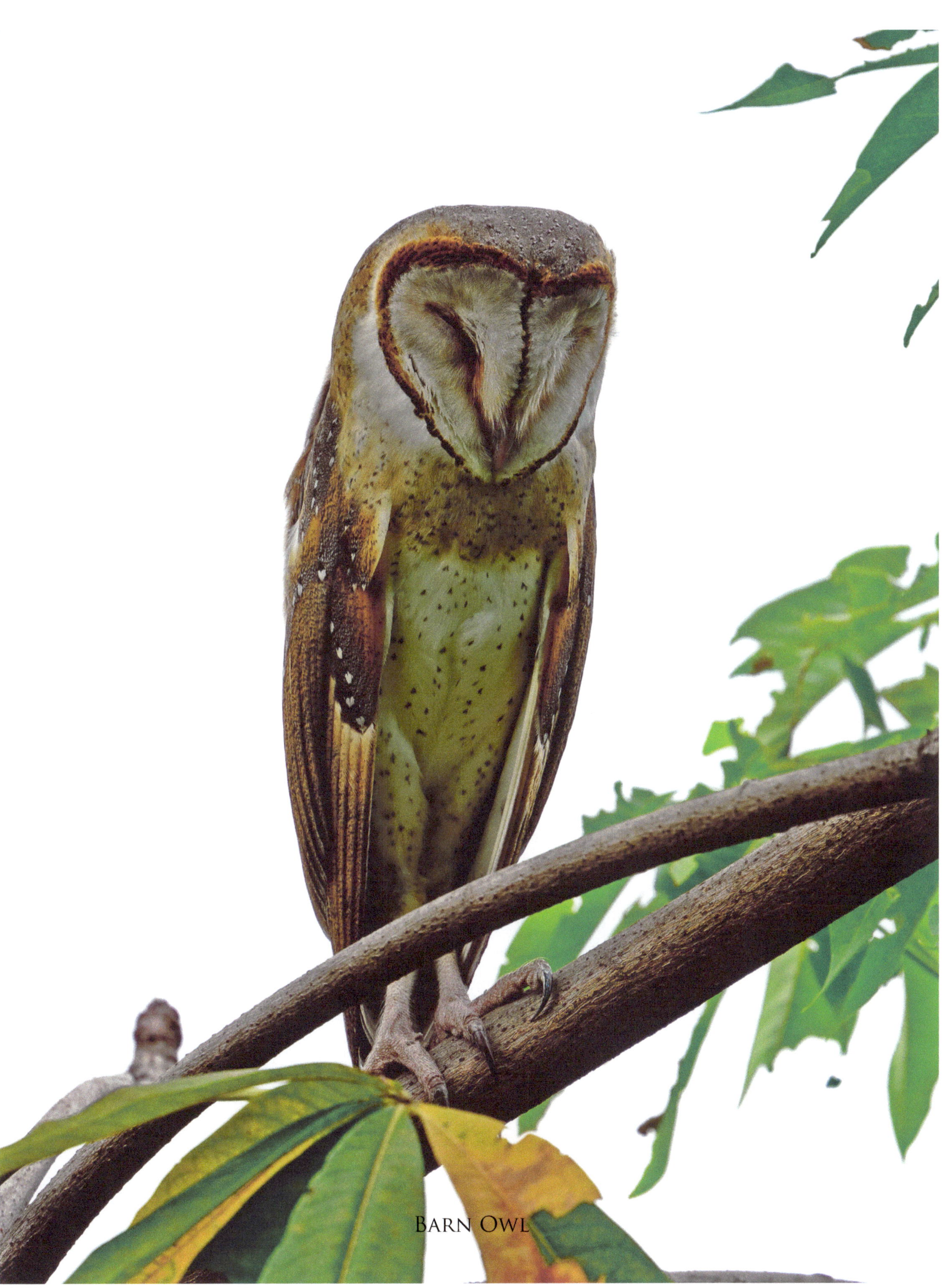

Barn Owl

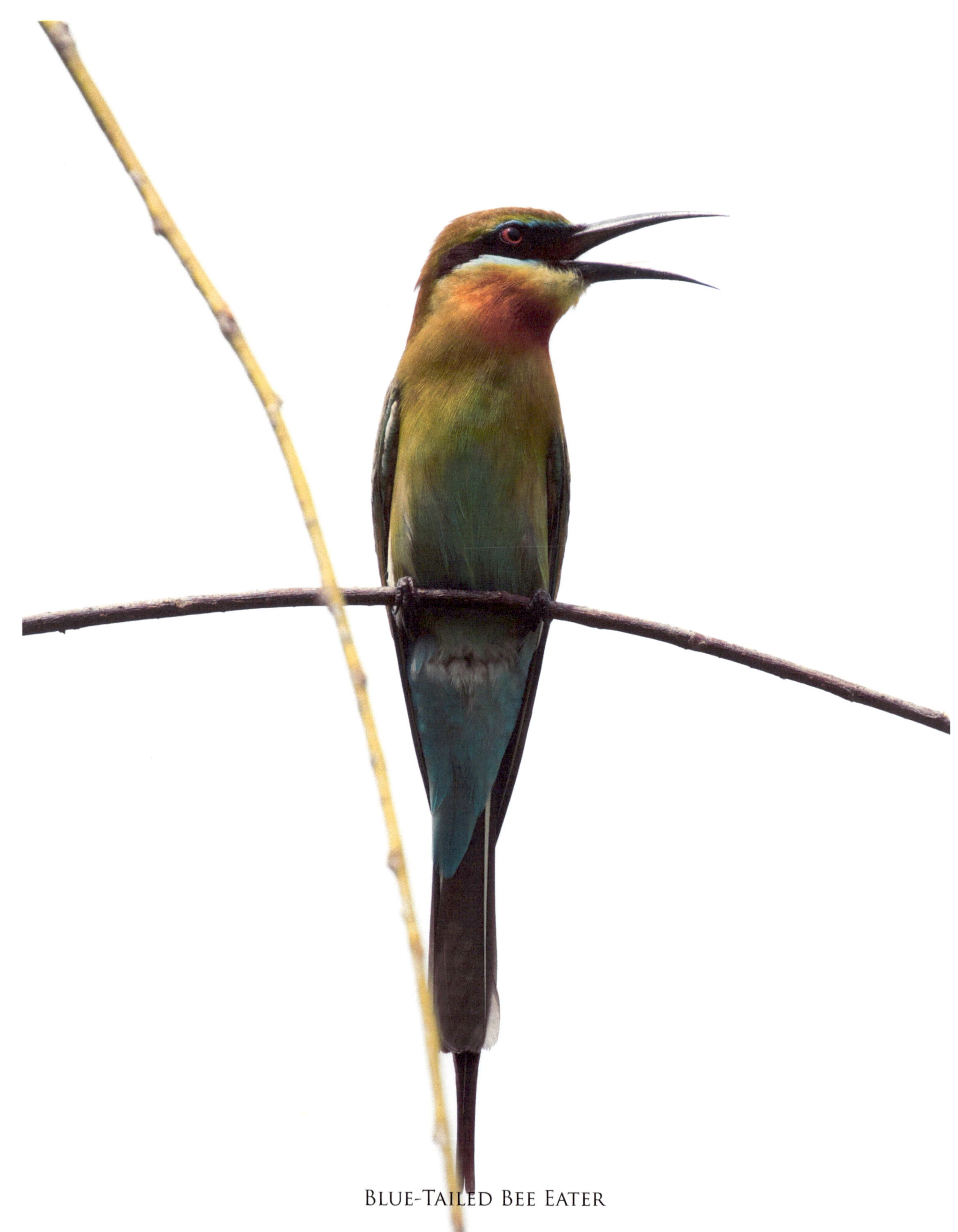

Blue-Tailed Bee Eater

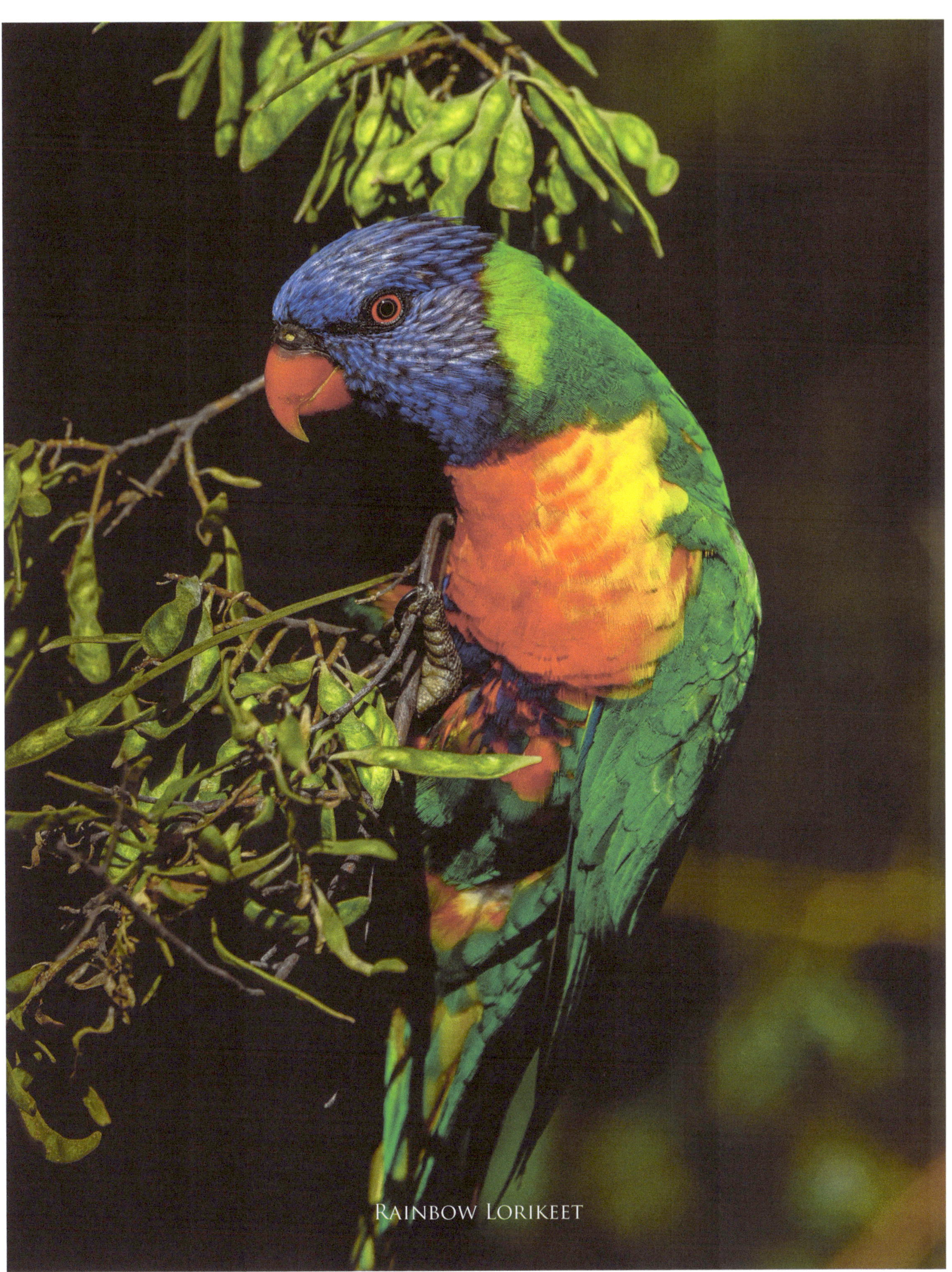
Rainbow Lorikeet

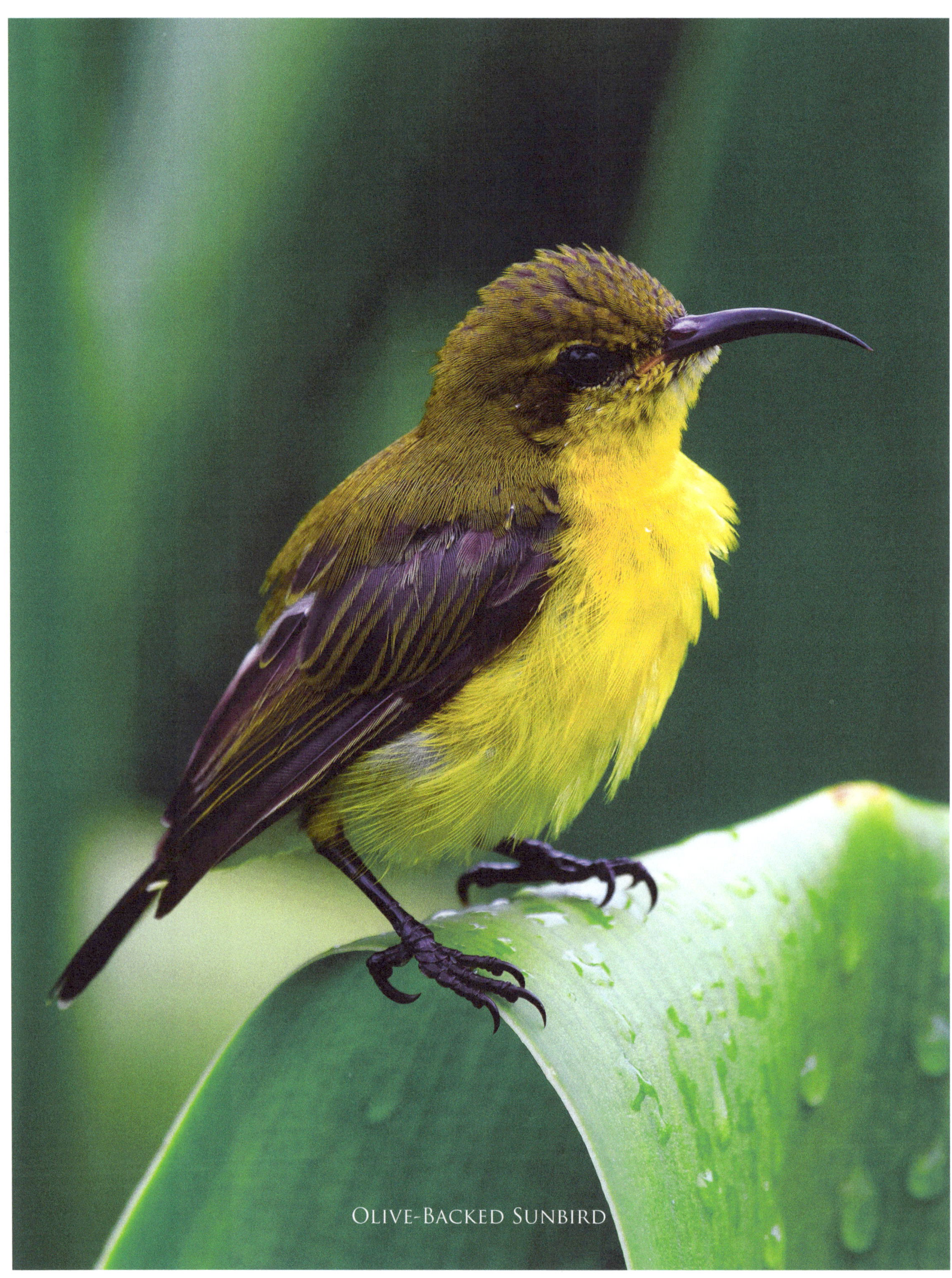

Olive-Backed Sunbird

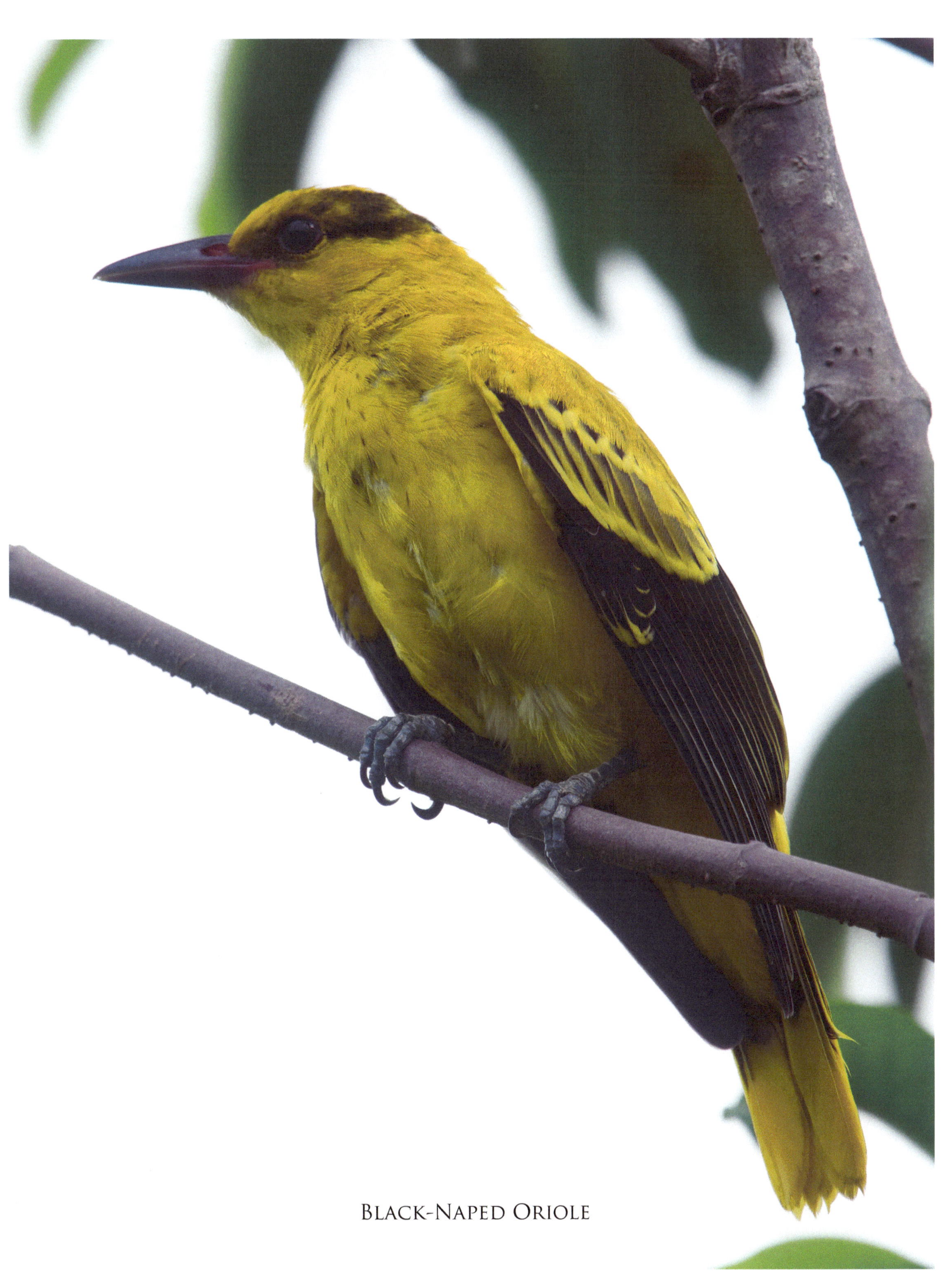

Black-Naped Oriole

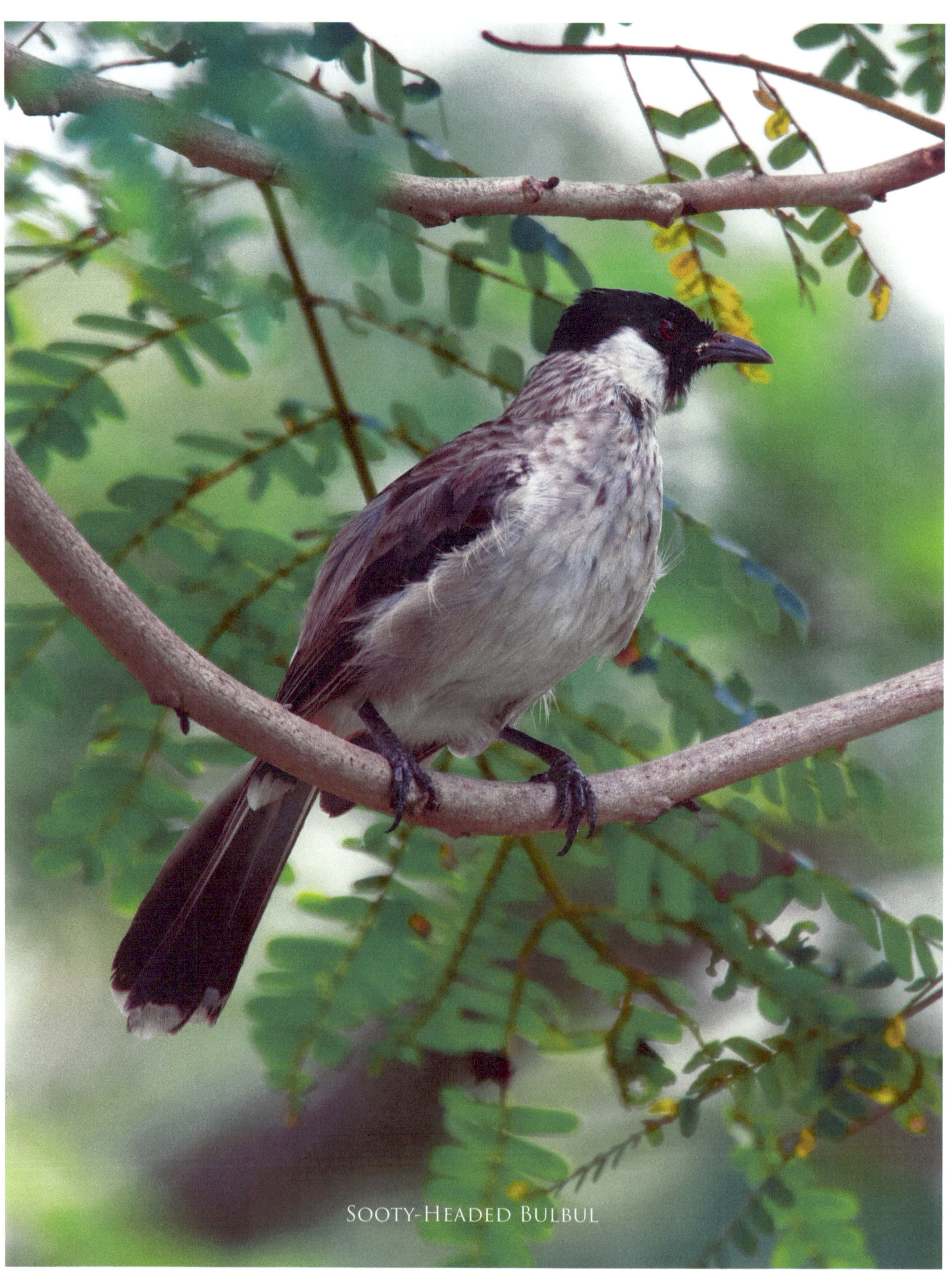

Sooty-Headed Bulbul

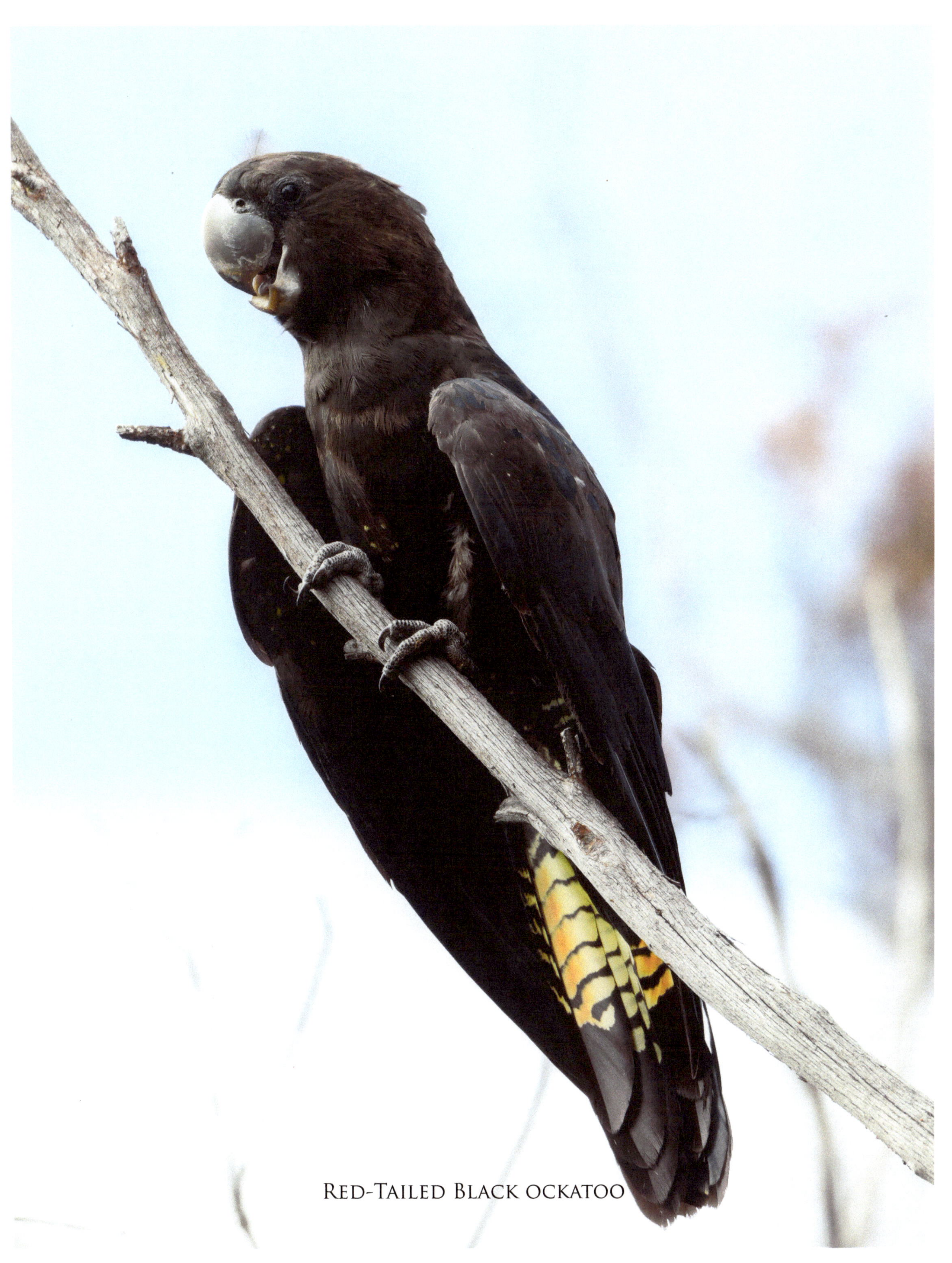

Red-Tailed Black ockatoo

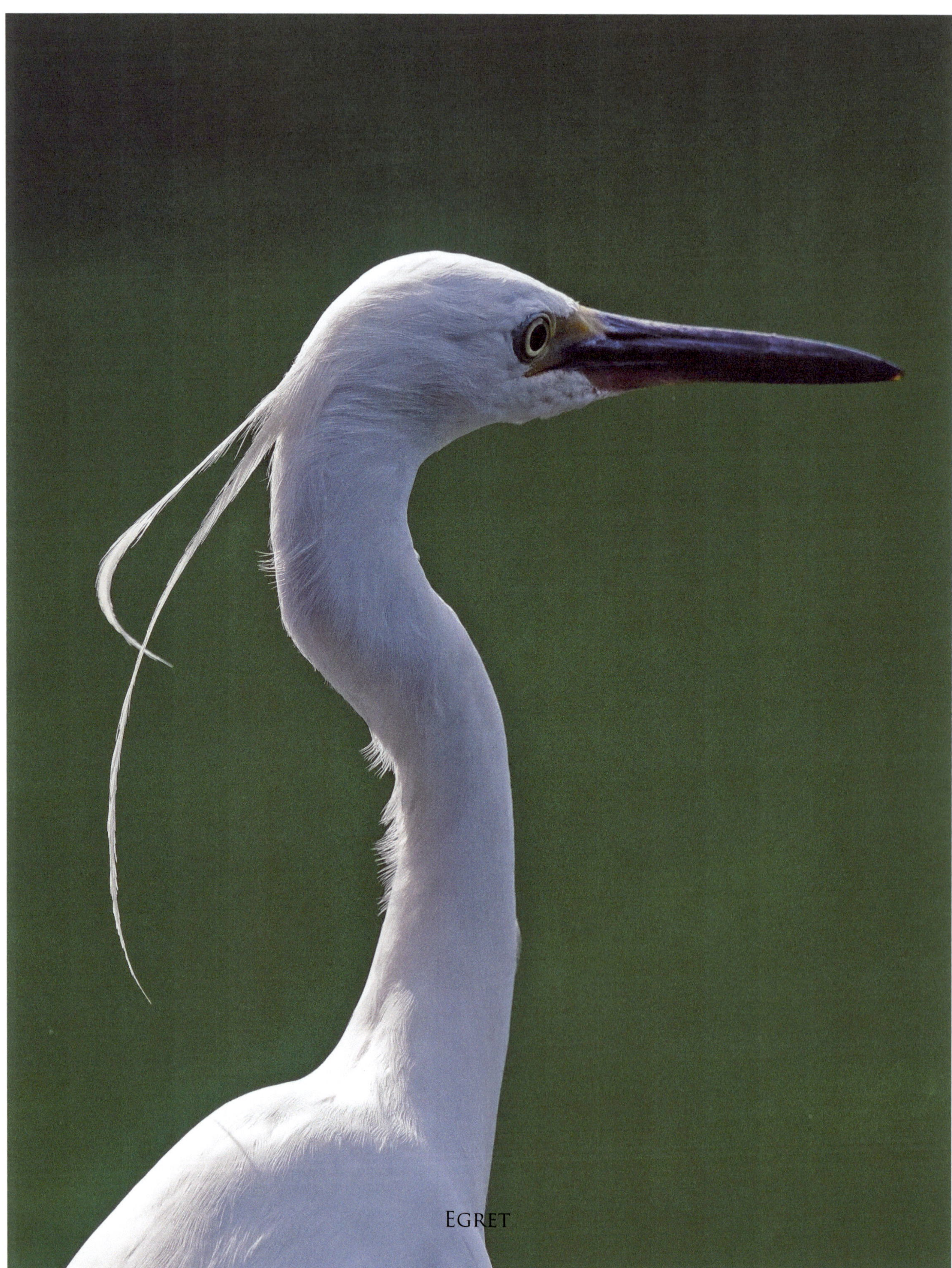

Egret

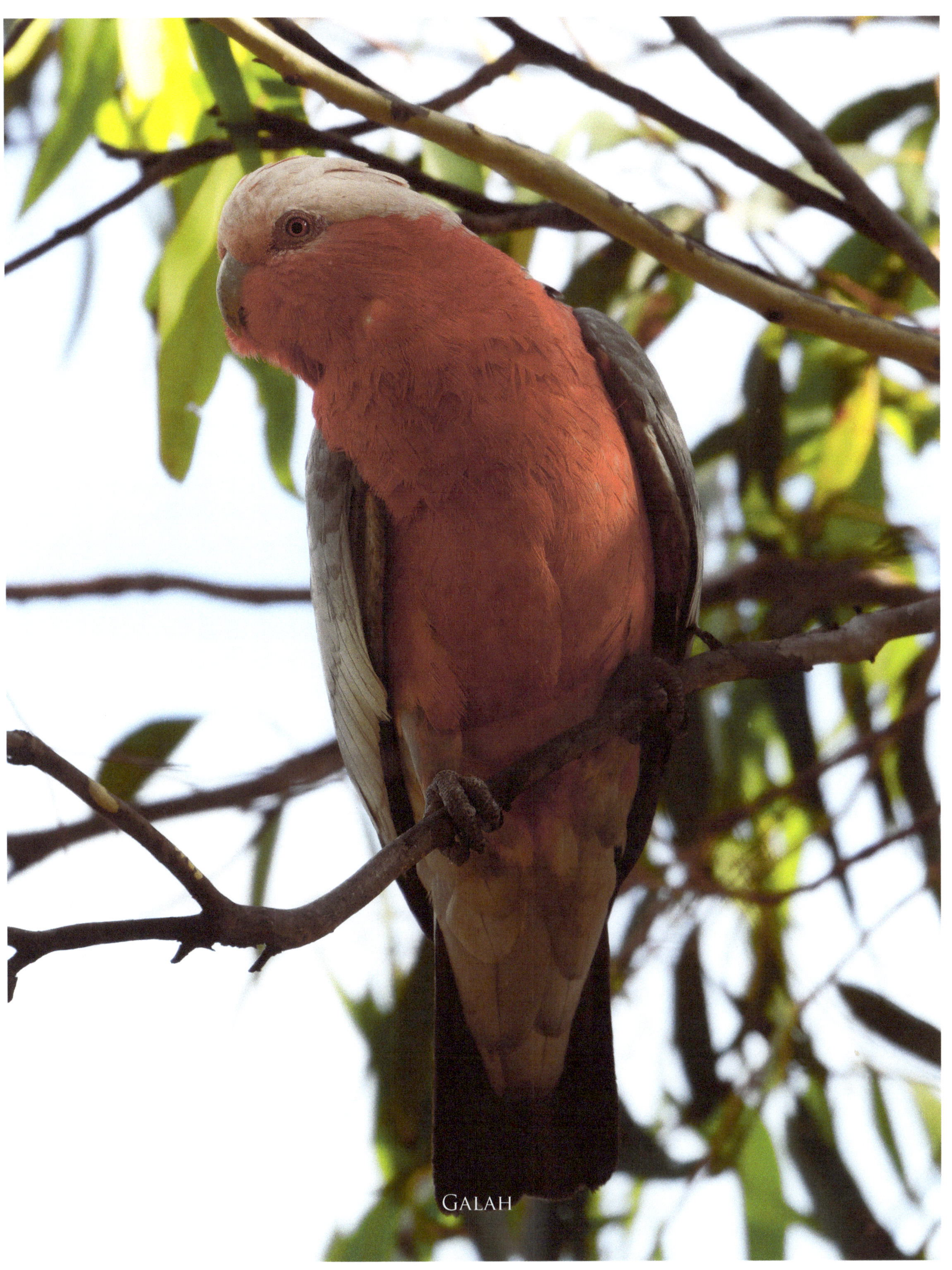
Galah

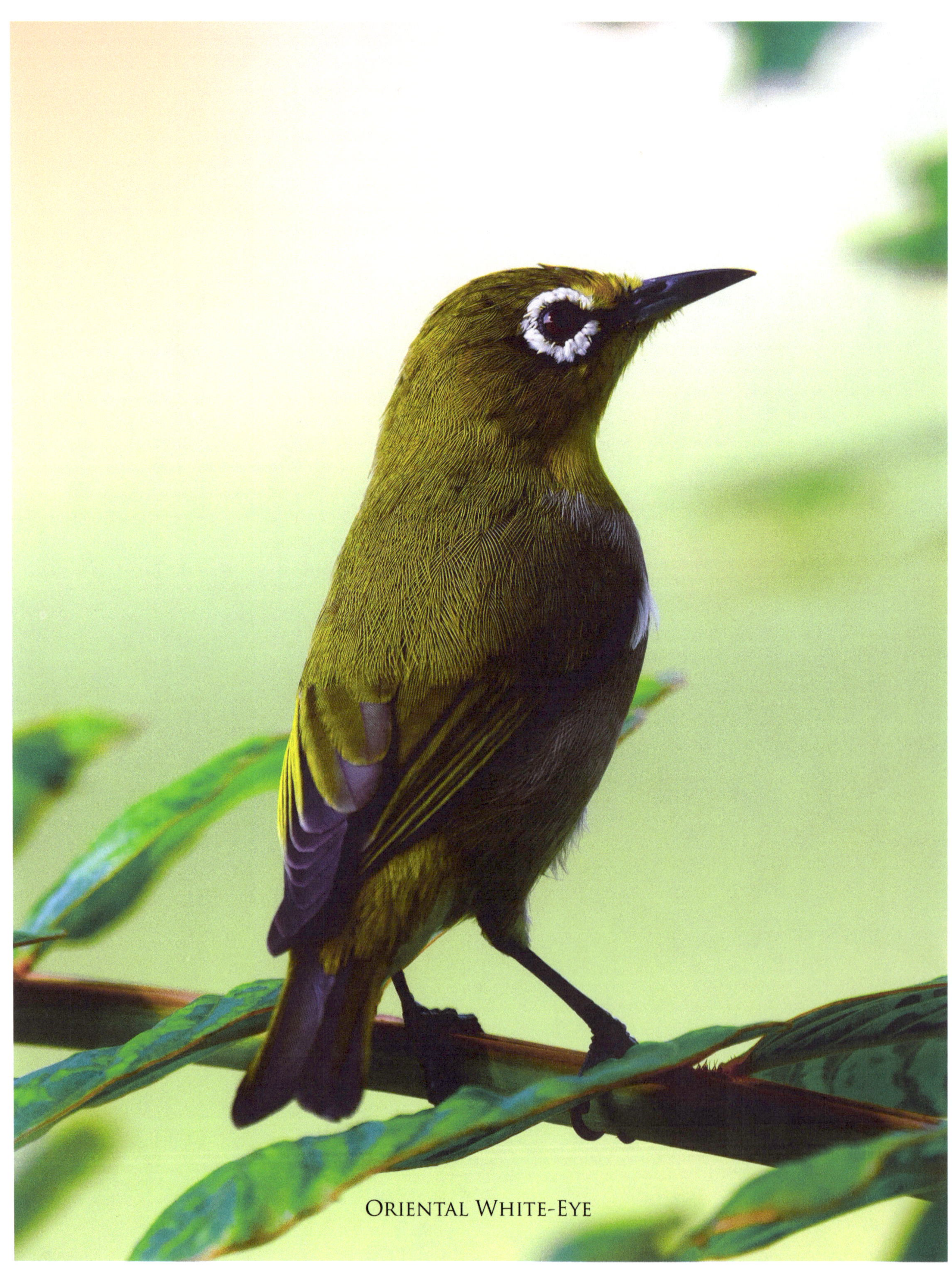

Oriental White-Eye

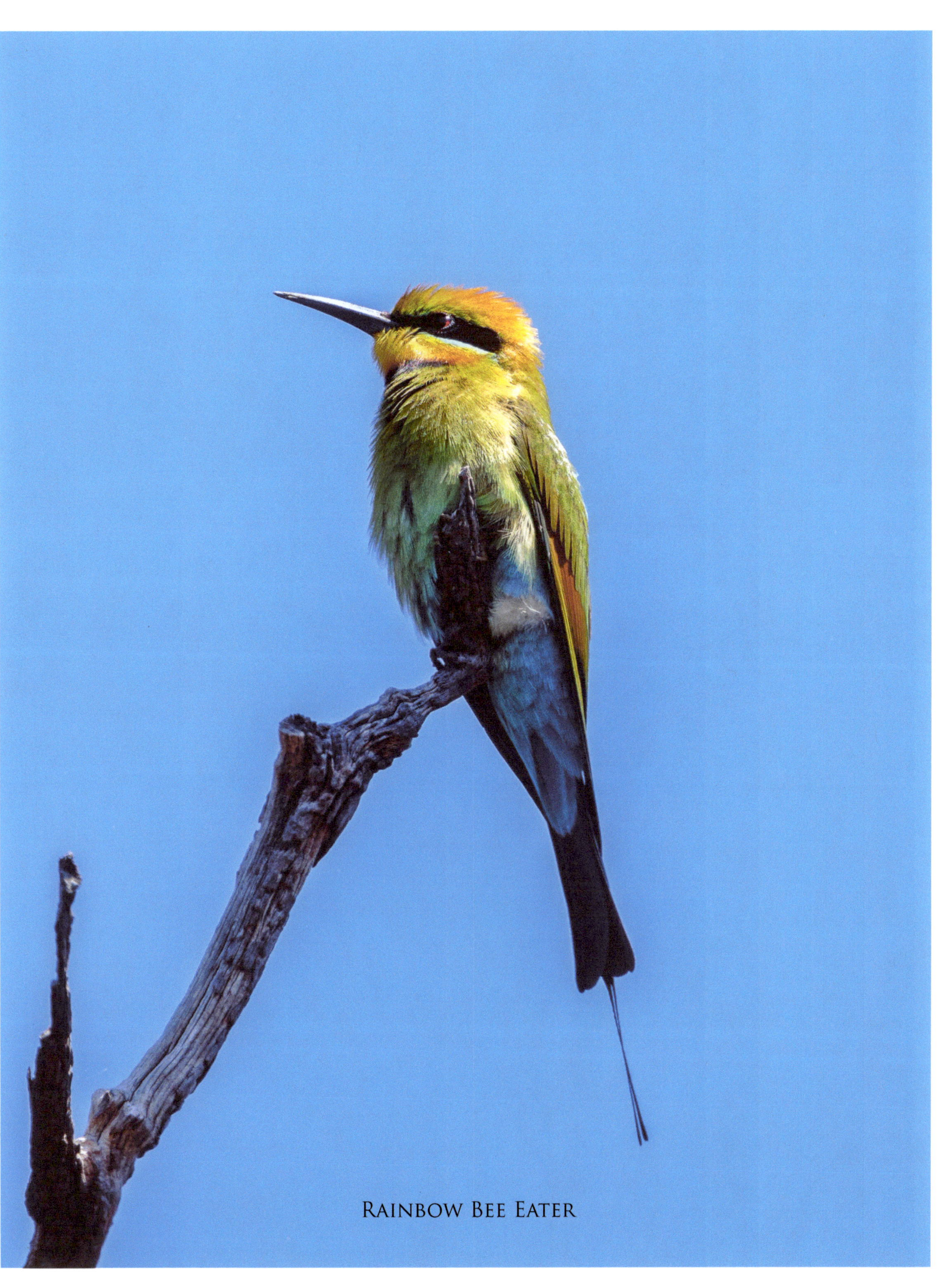
Rainbow Bee Eater

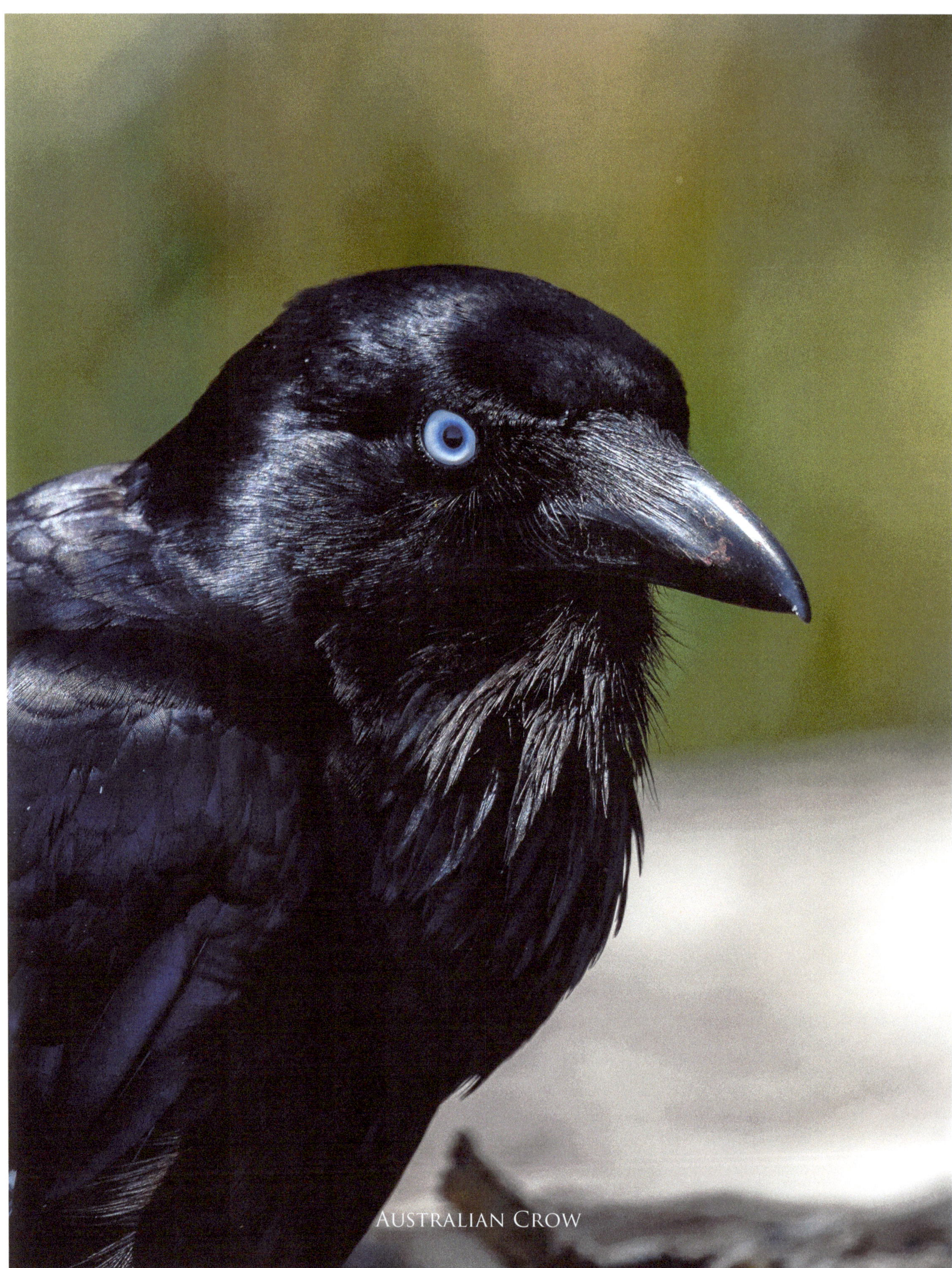
Australian Crow

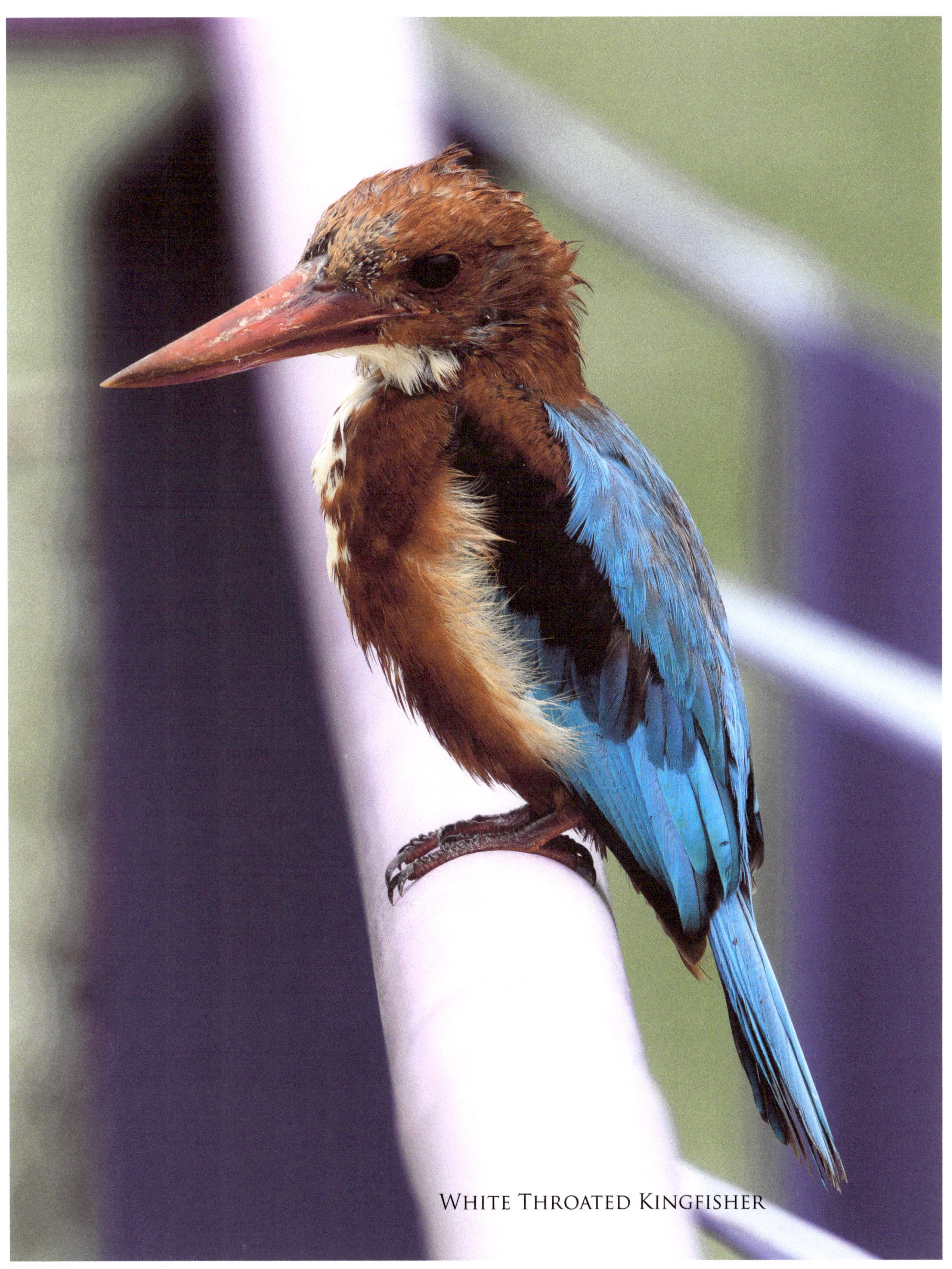

White Throated Kingfisher

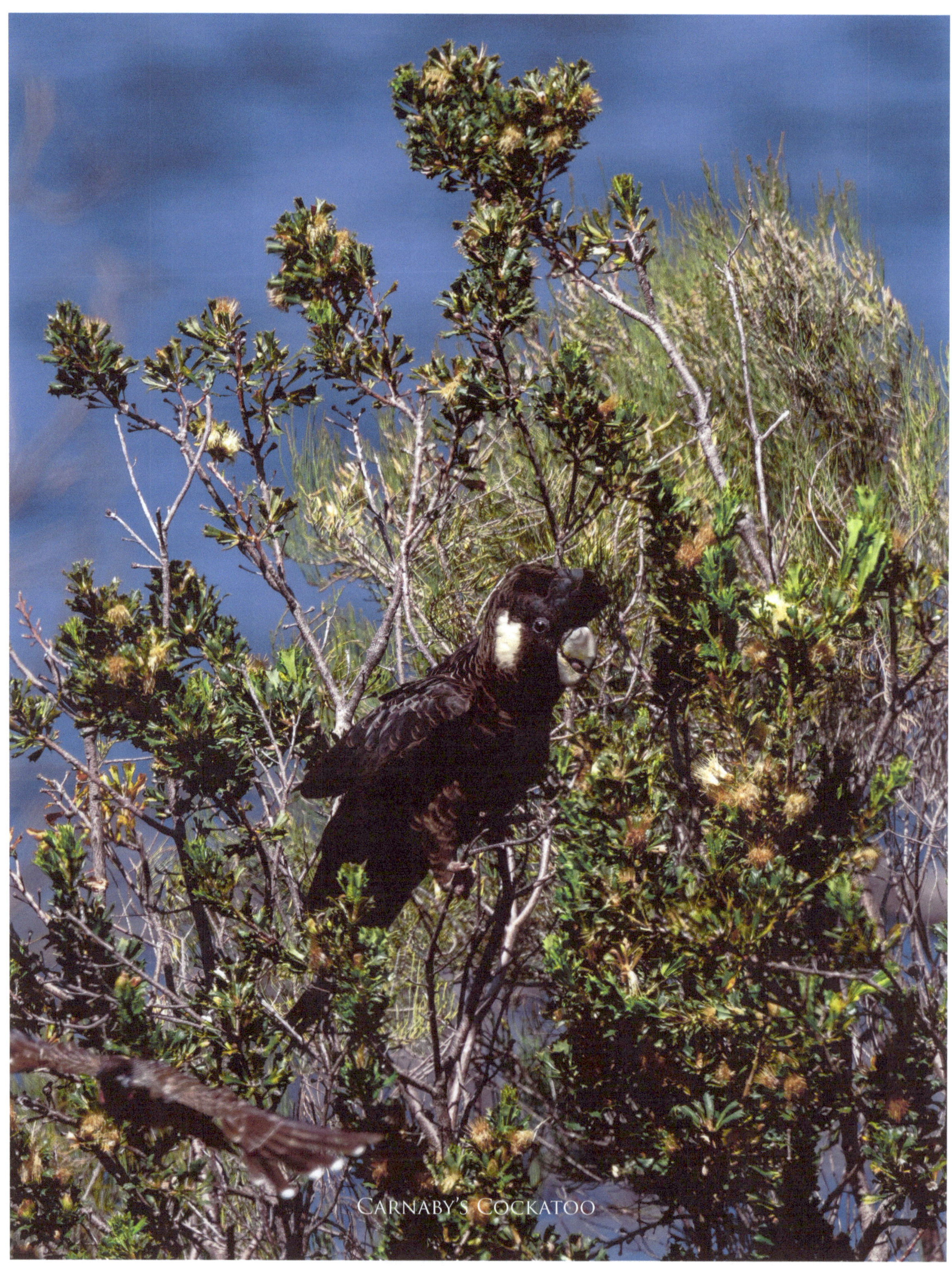

Carnaby's Cockatoo

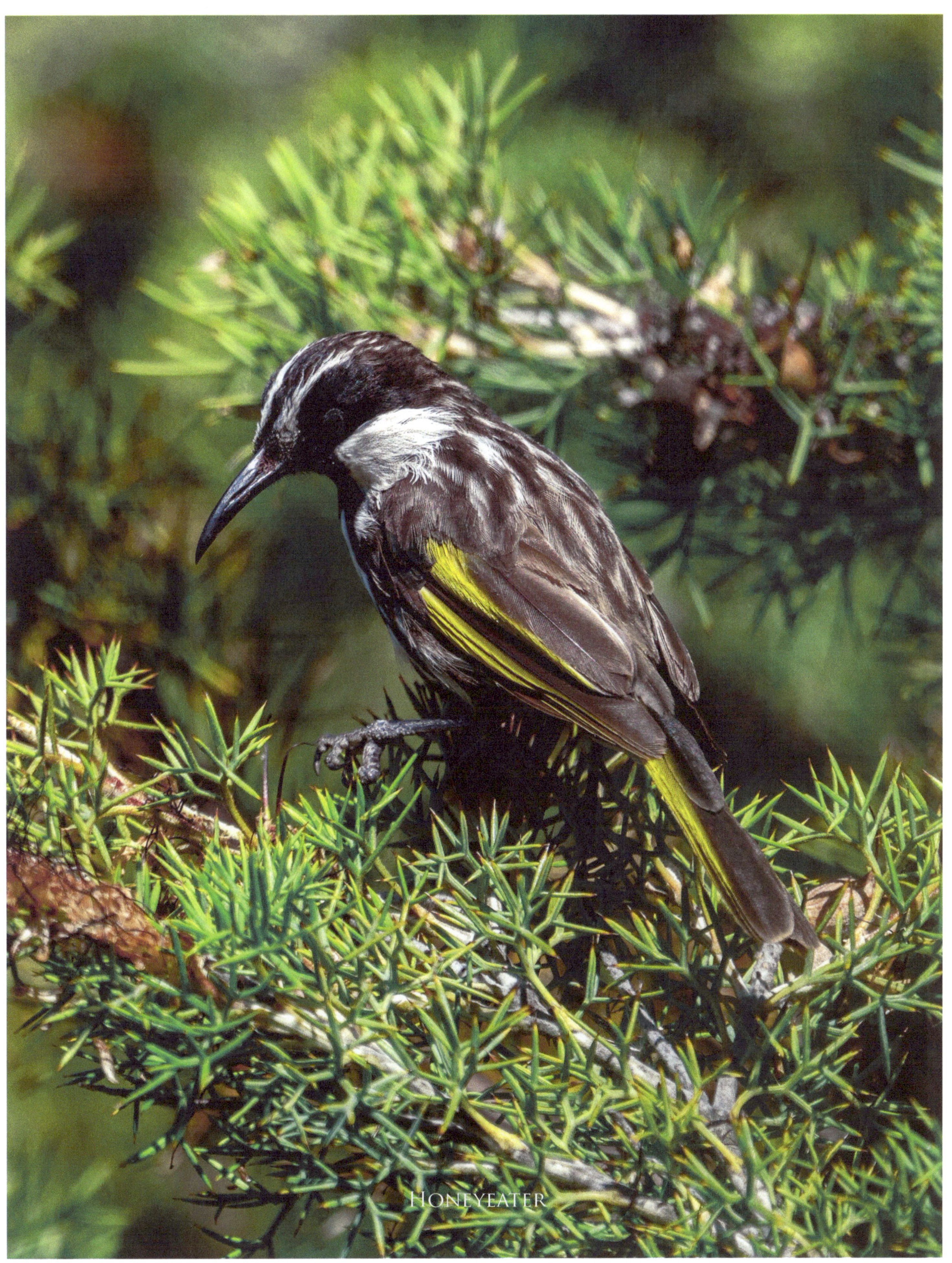

Honeyeater

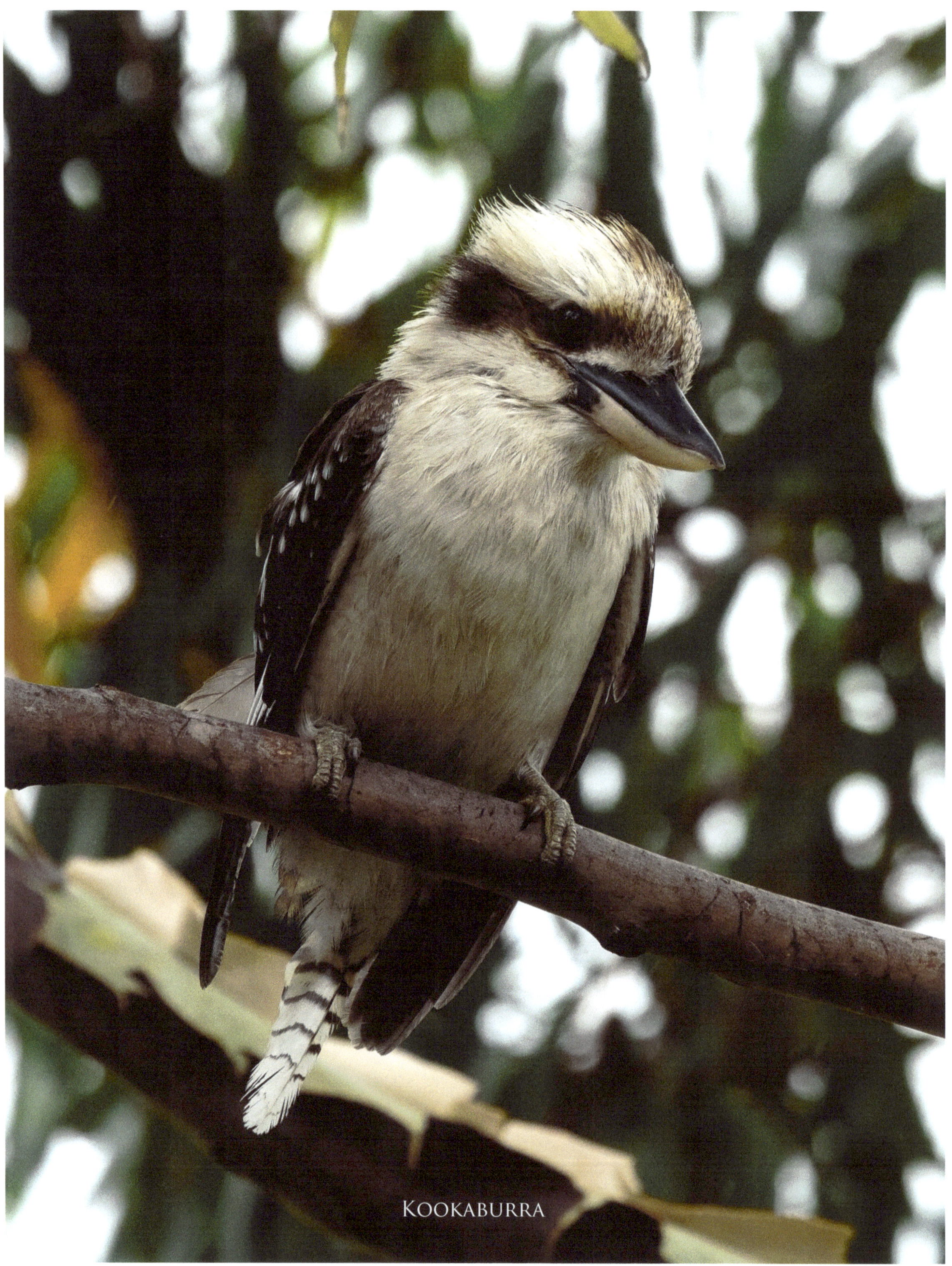

Kookaburra

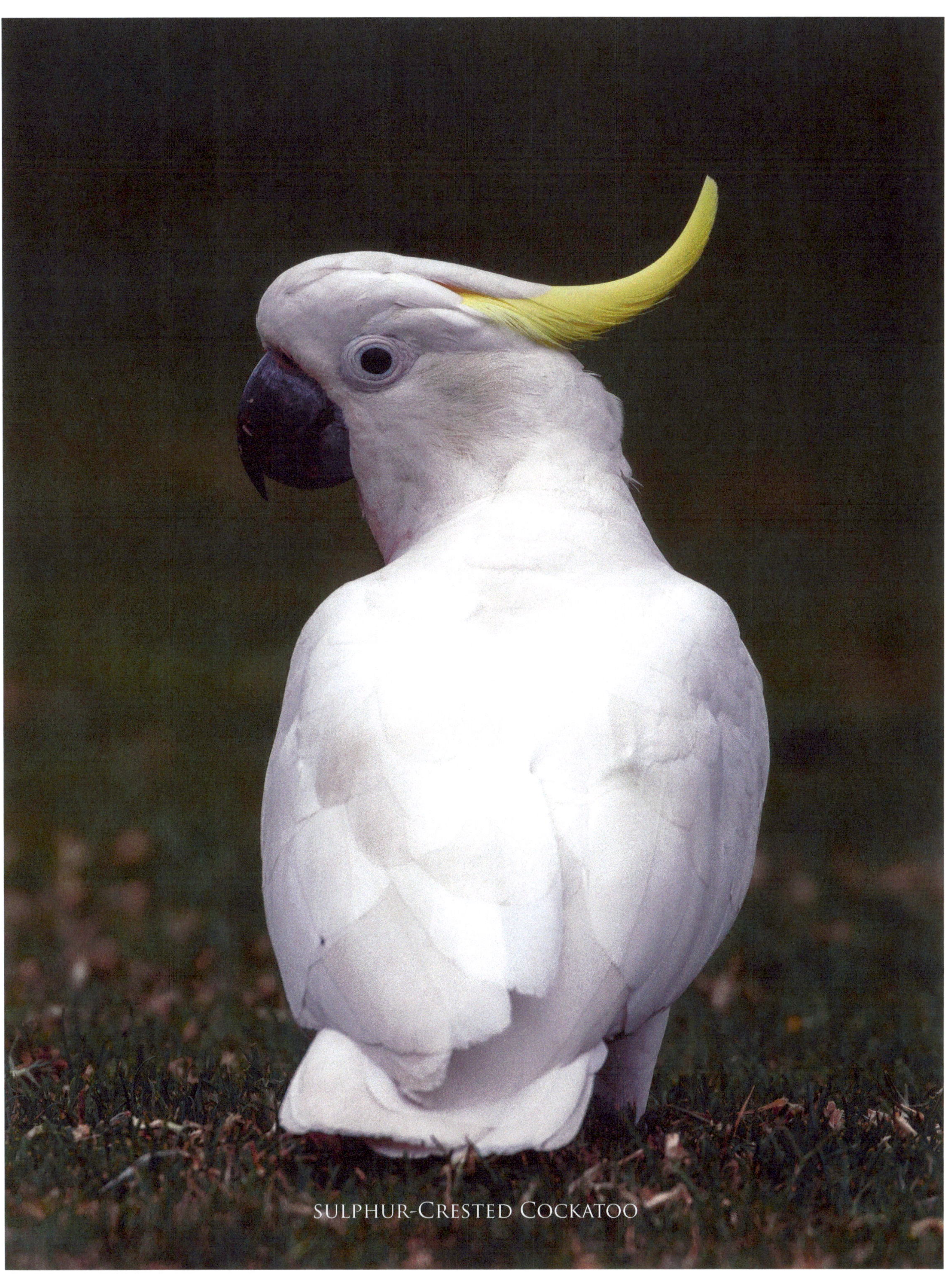

Sulphur-Crested Cockatoo

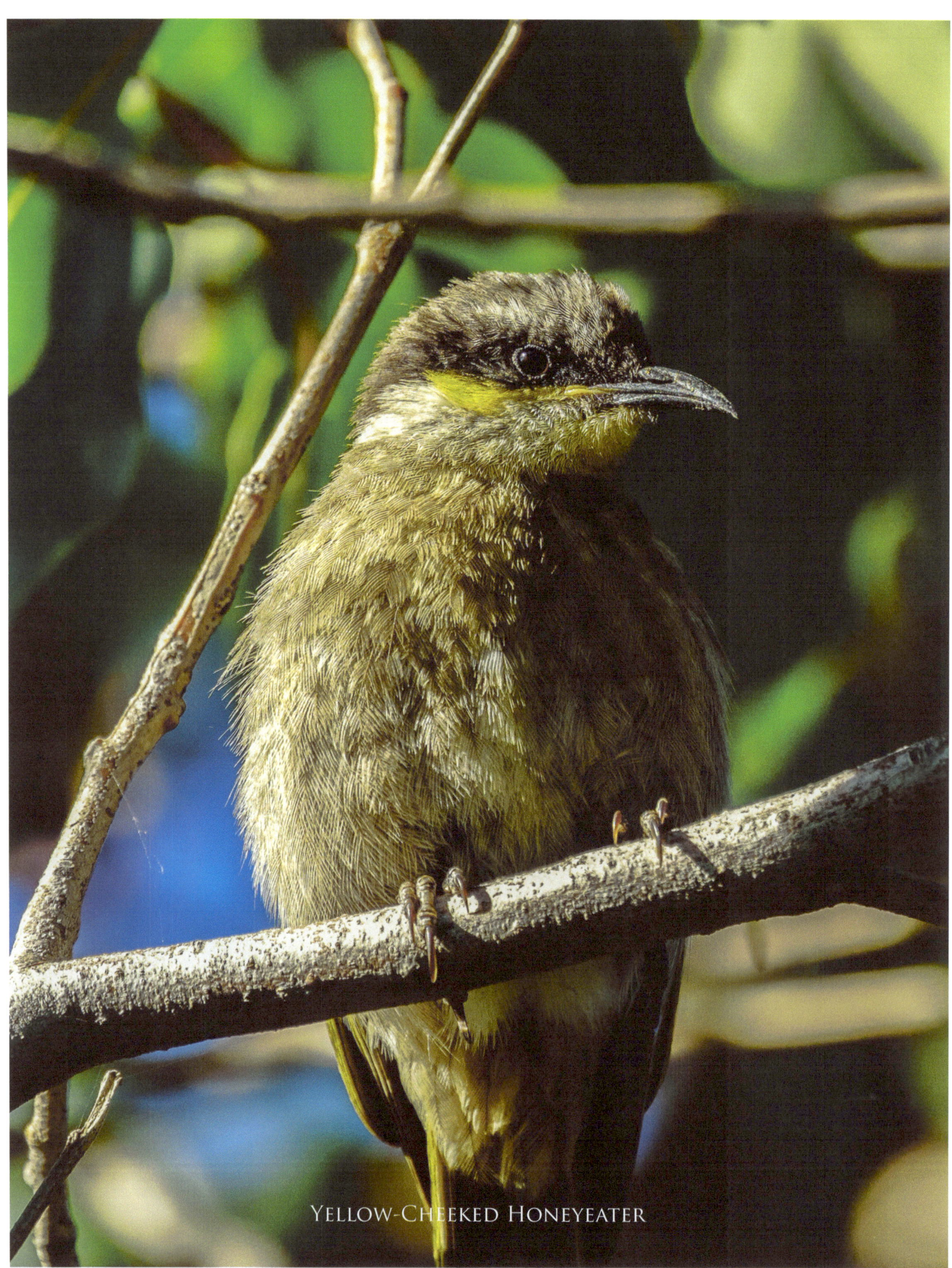

Yellow-Cheeked Honeyeater

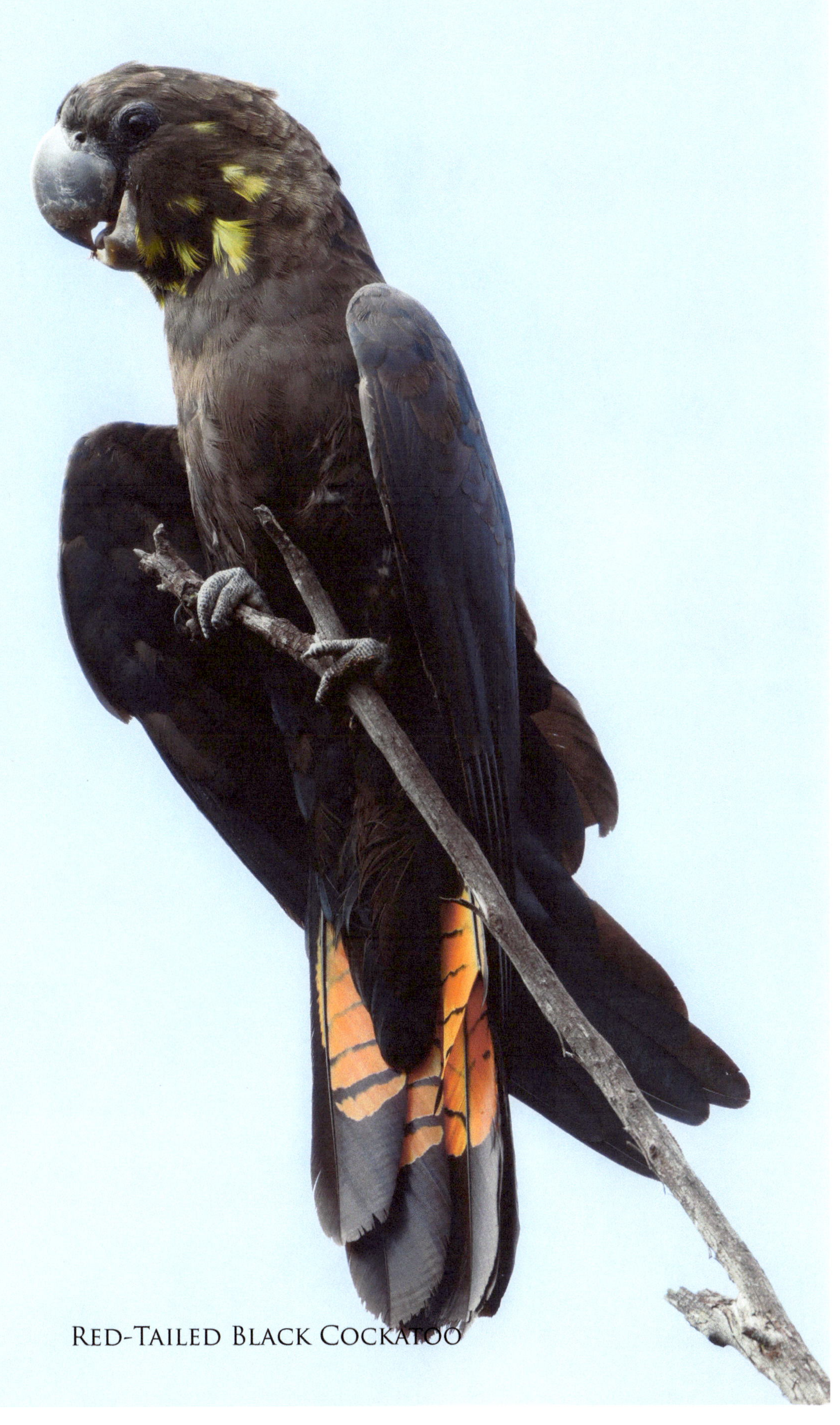

Red-Tailed Black Cockatoo

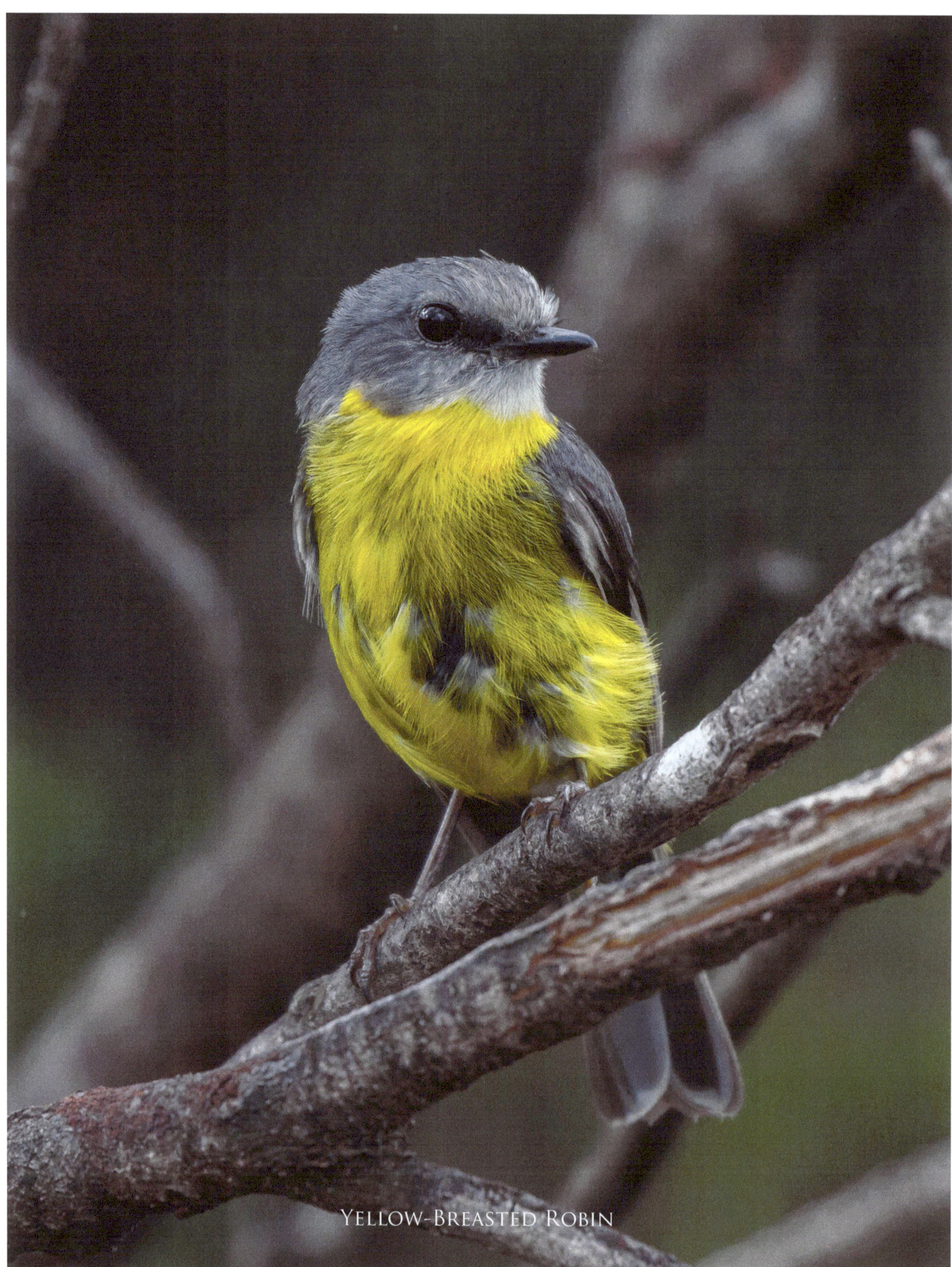
Yellow-Breasted Robin

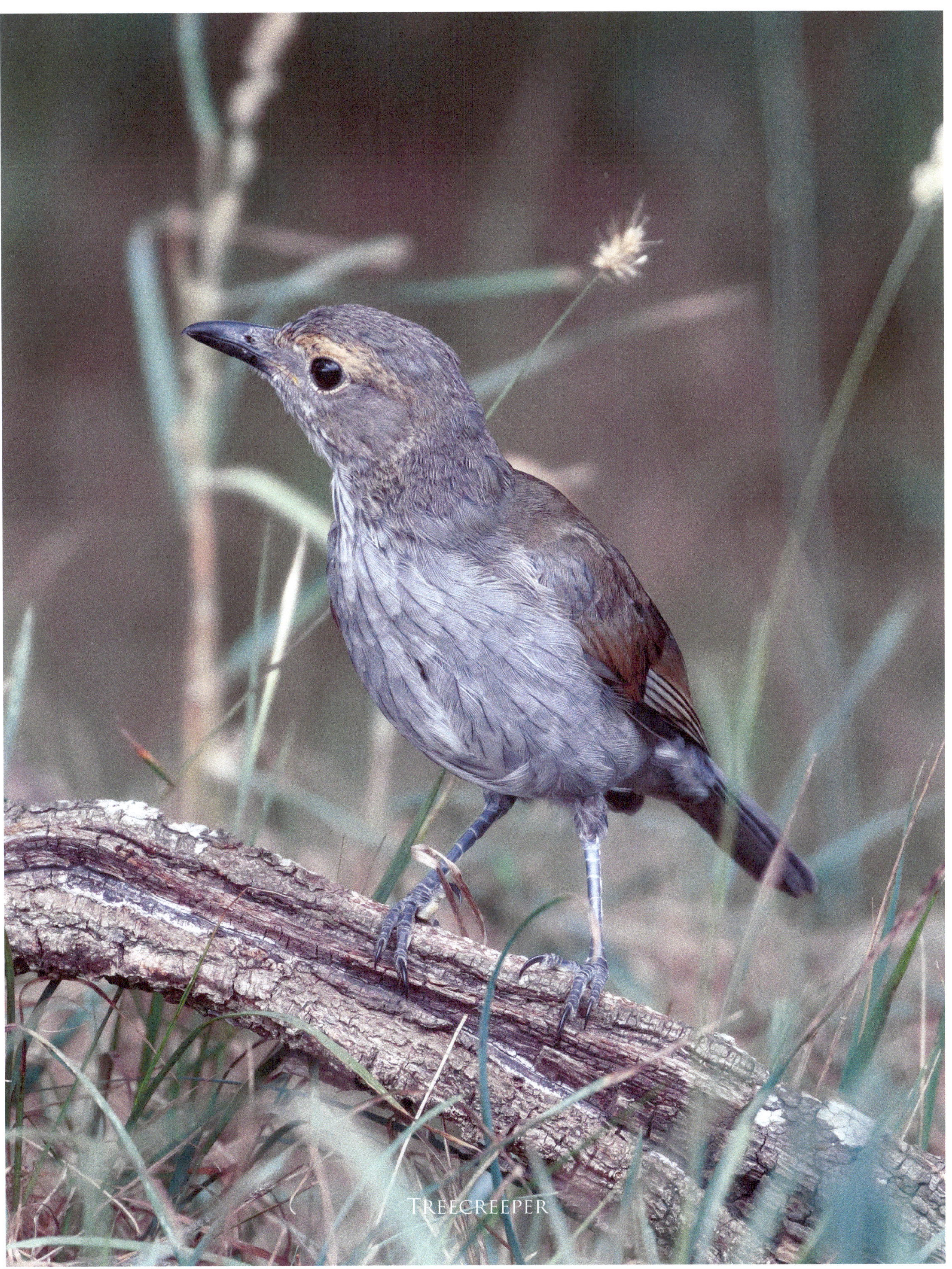

Treecreeper

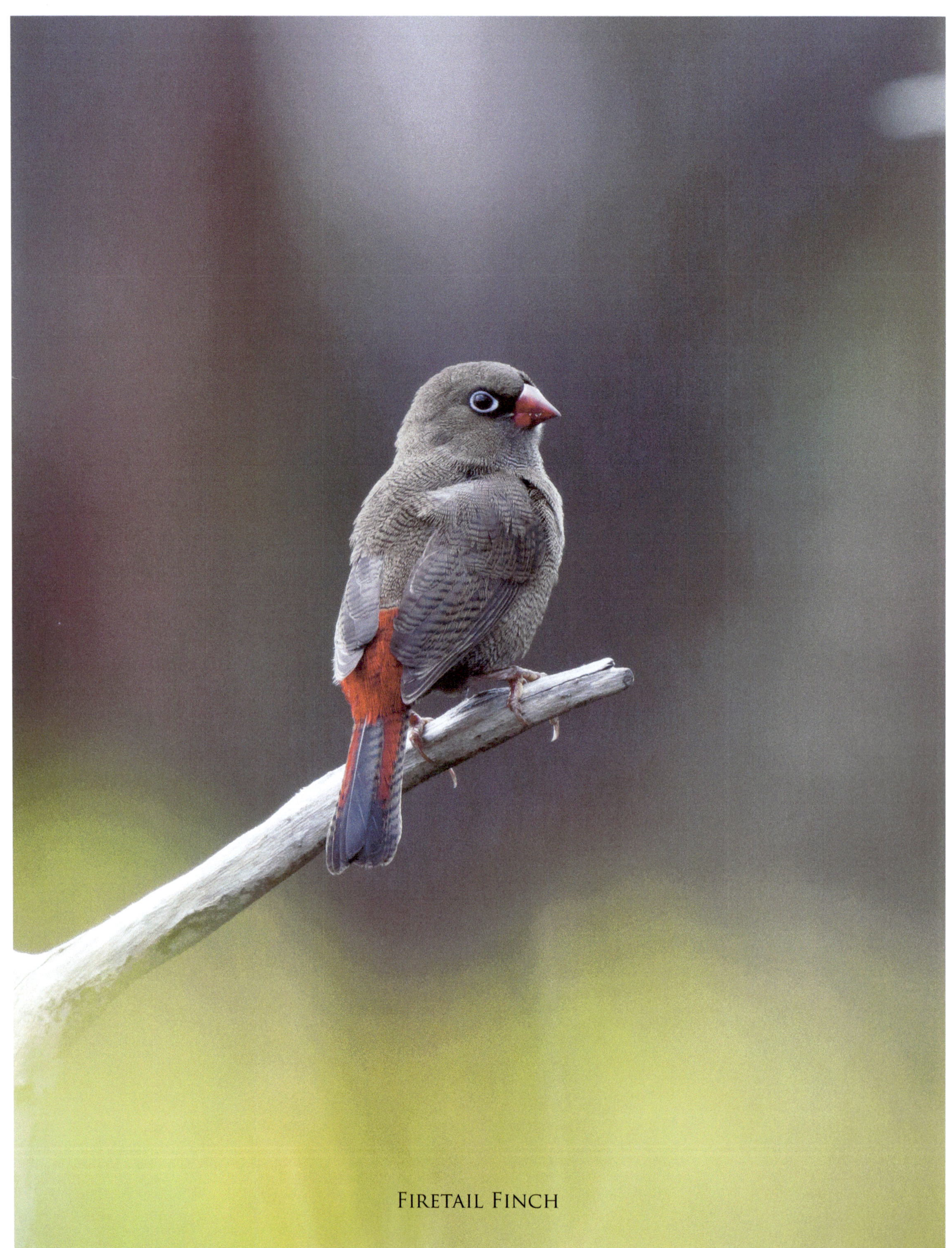

Firetail Finch

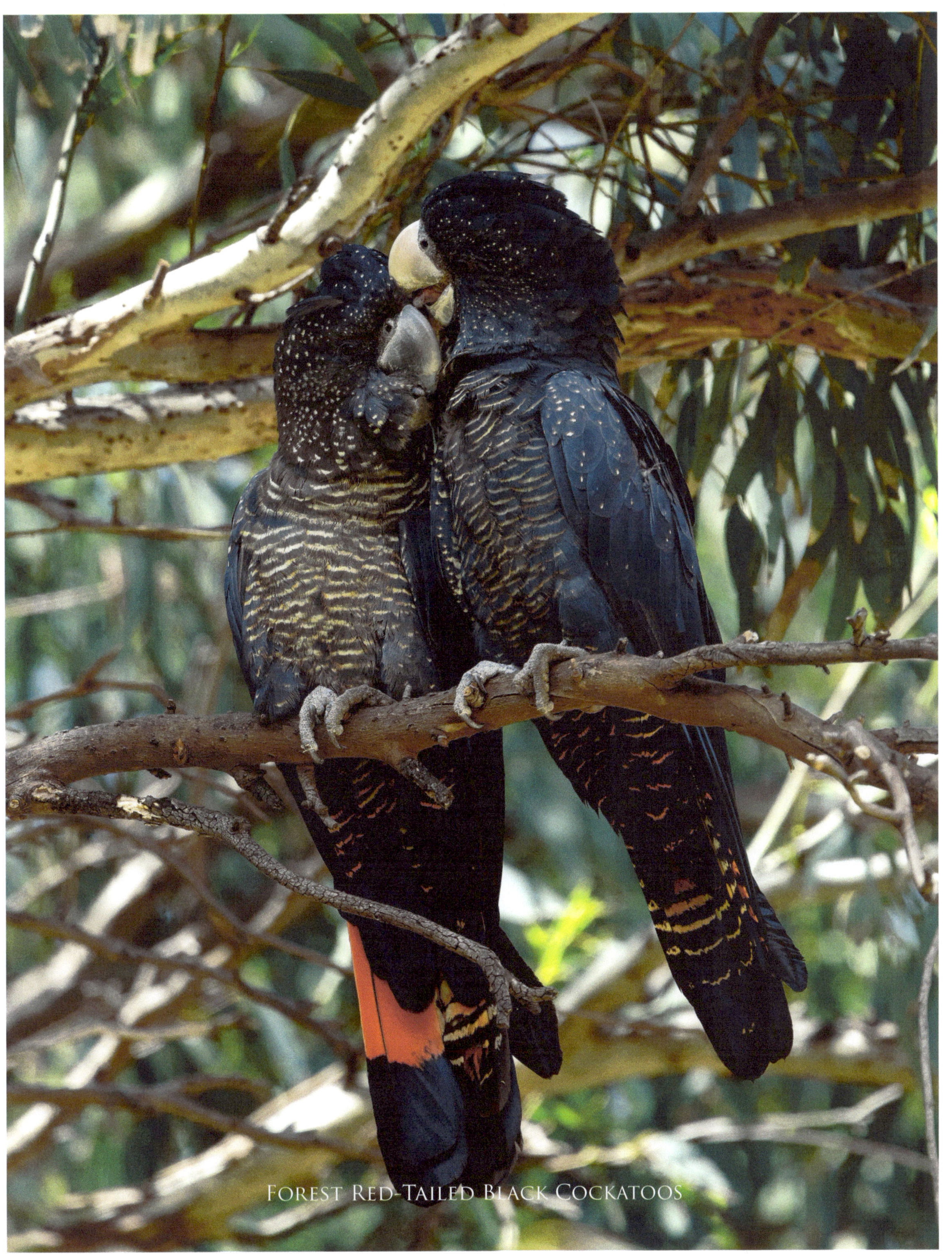

Forest Red-Tailed Black Cockatoos

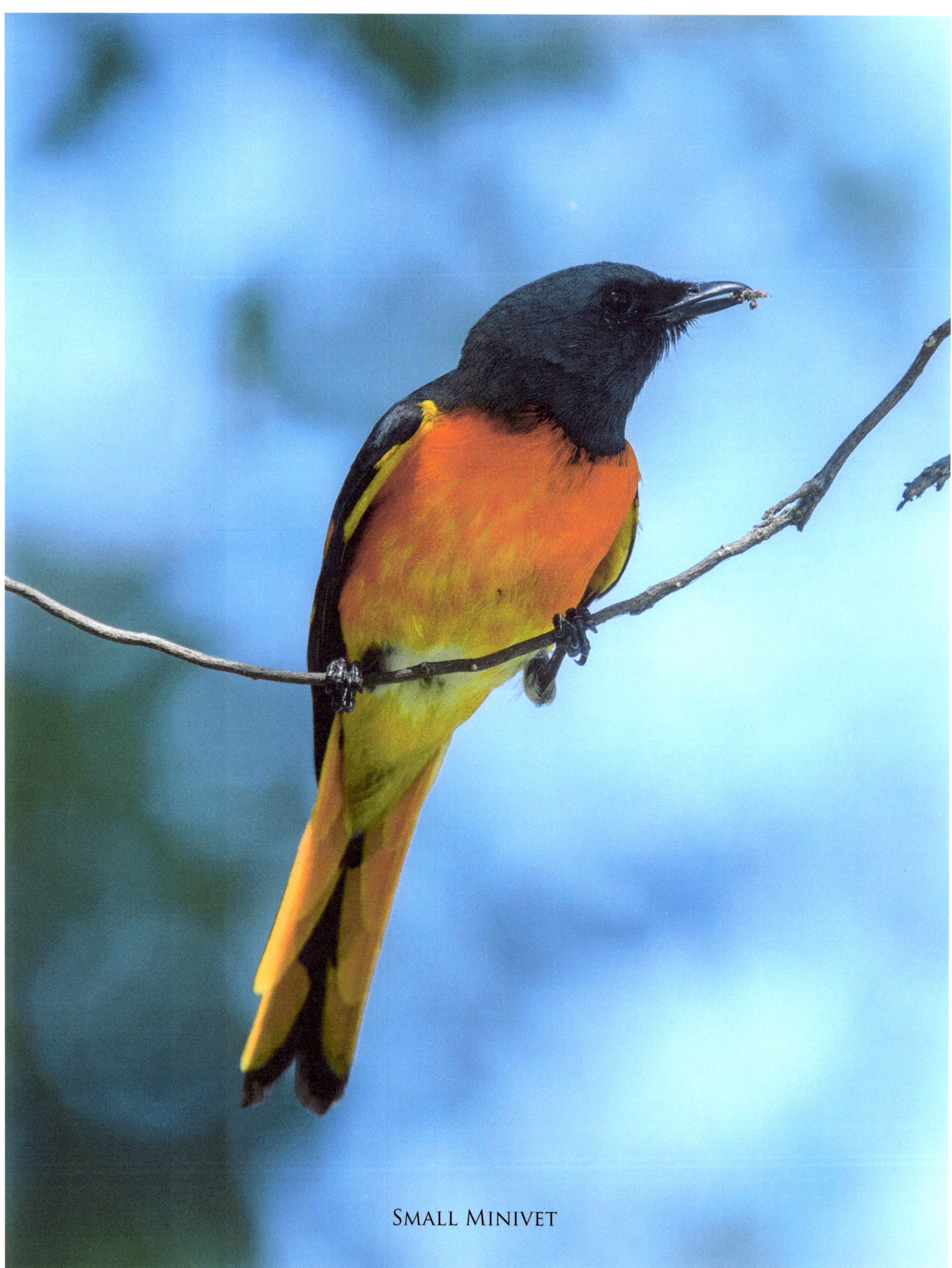

Small Minivet

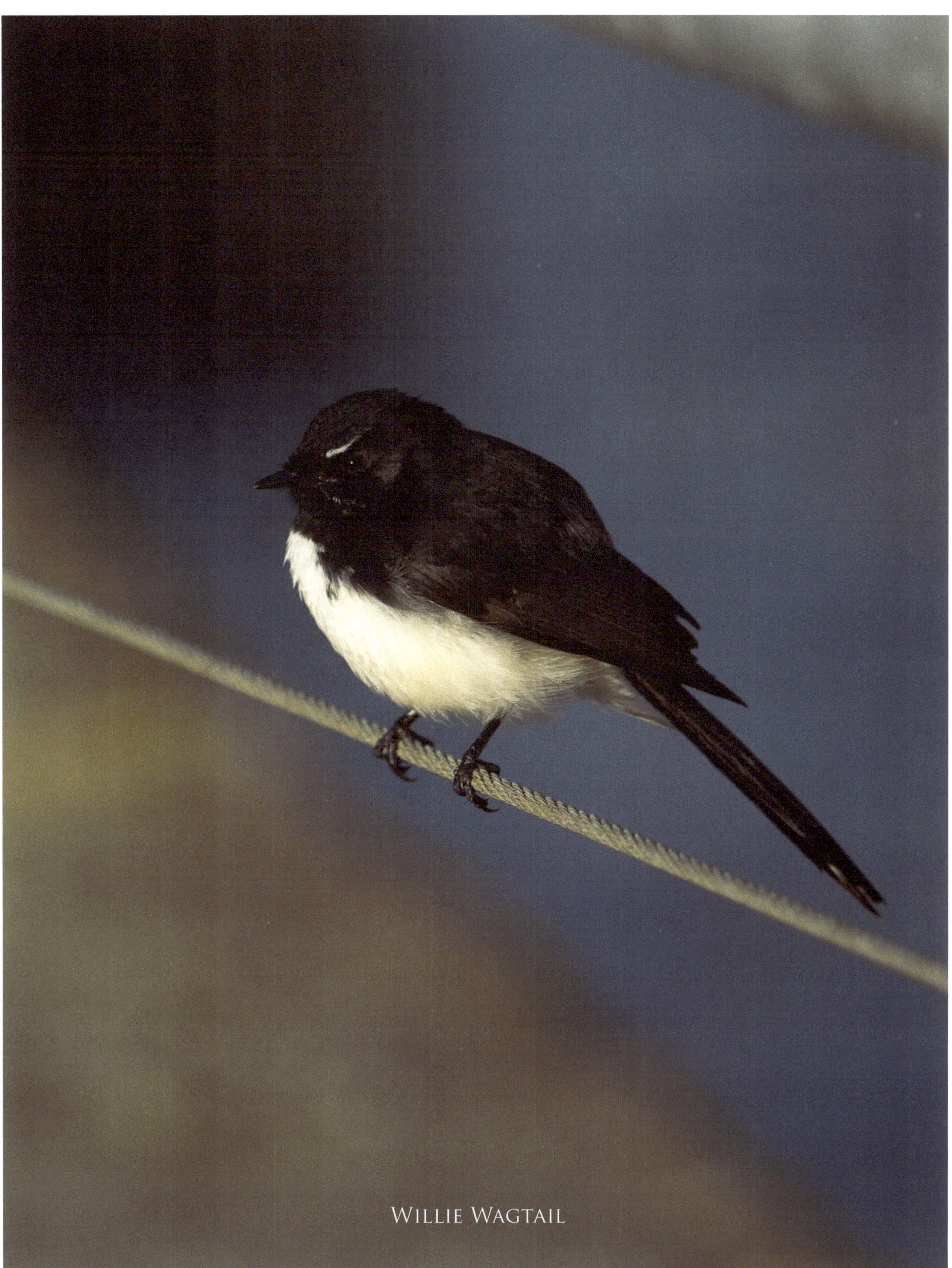

Willie Wagtail

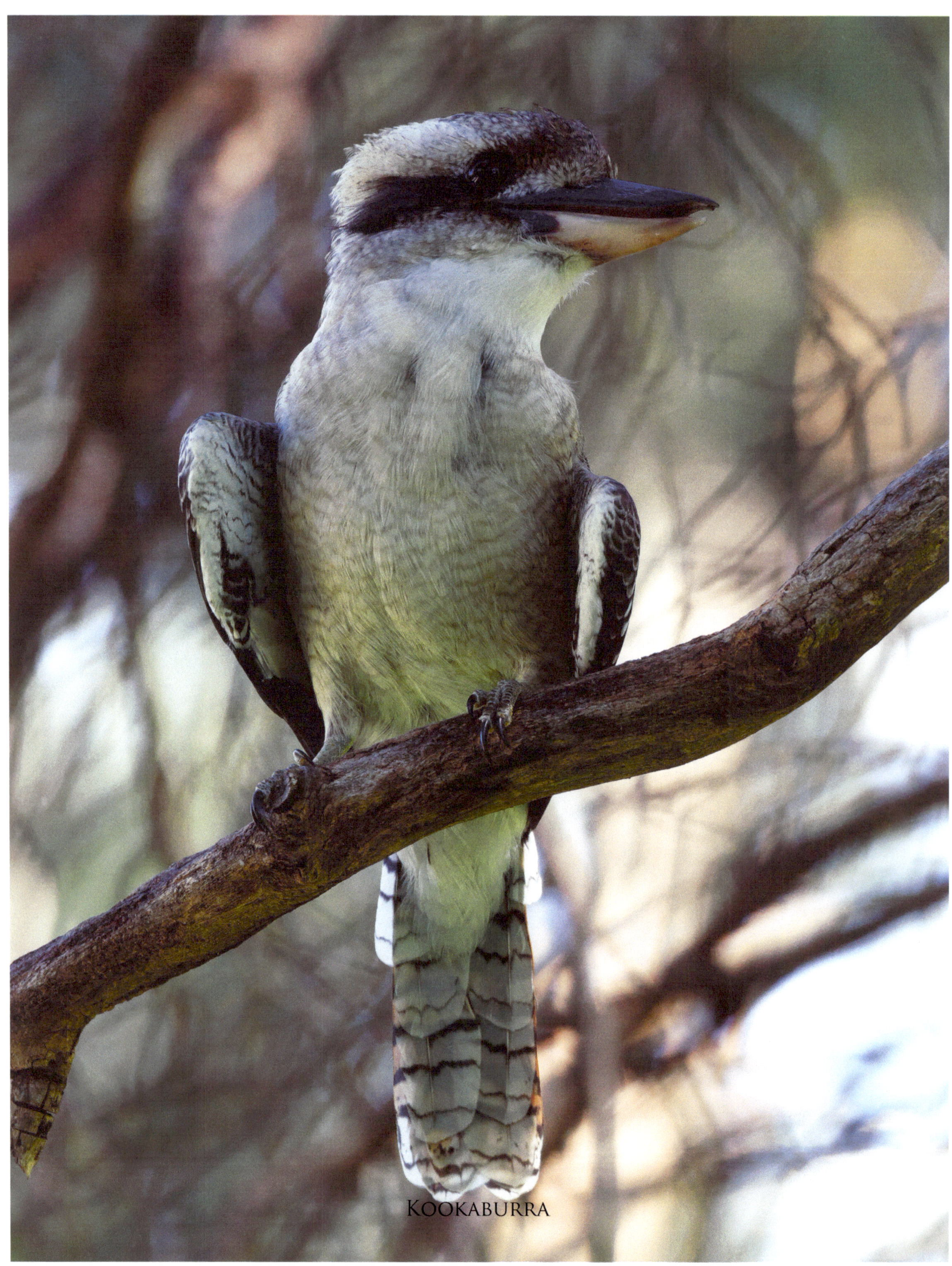

Kookaburra

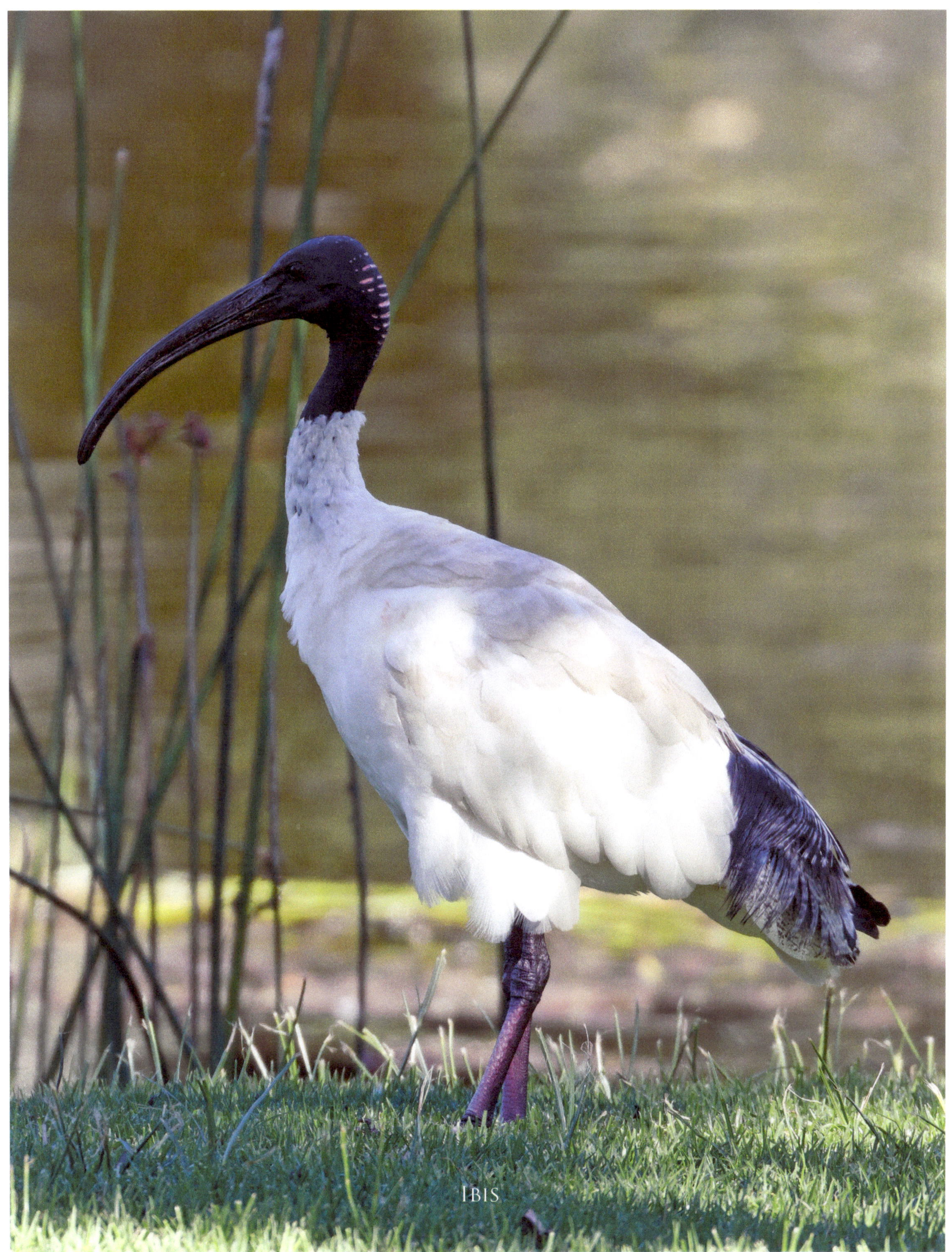

Ibis

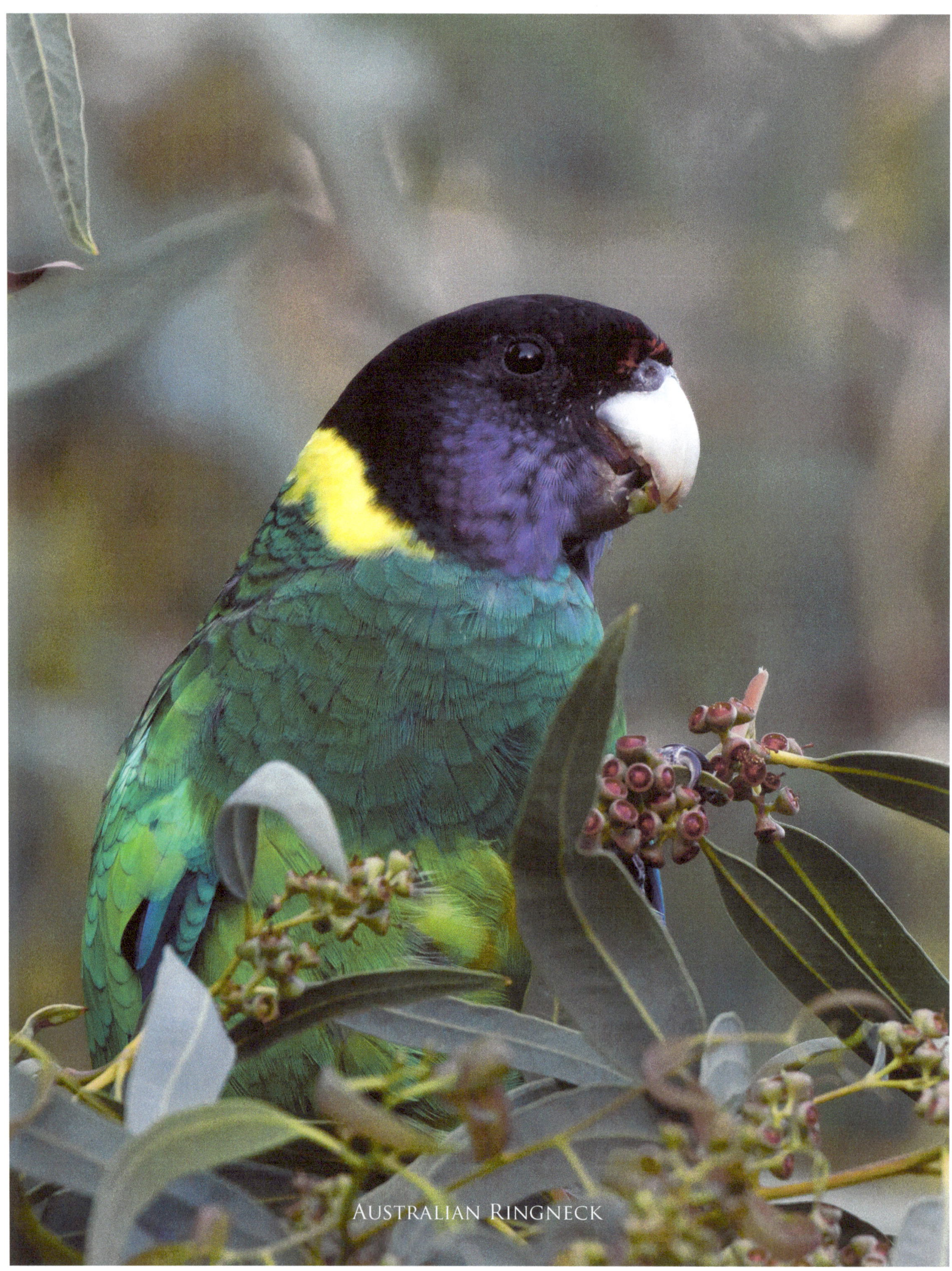

Australian Ringneck

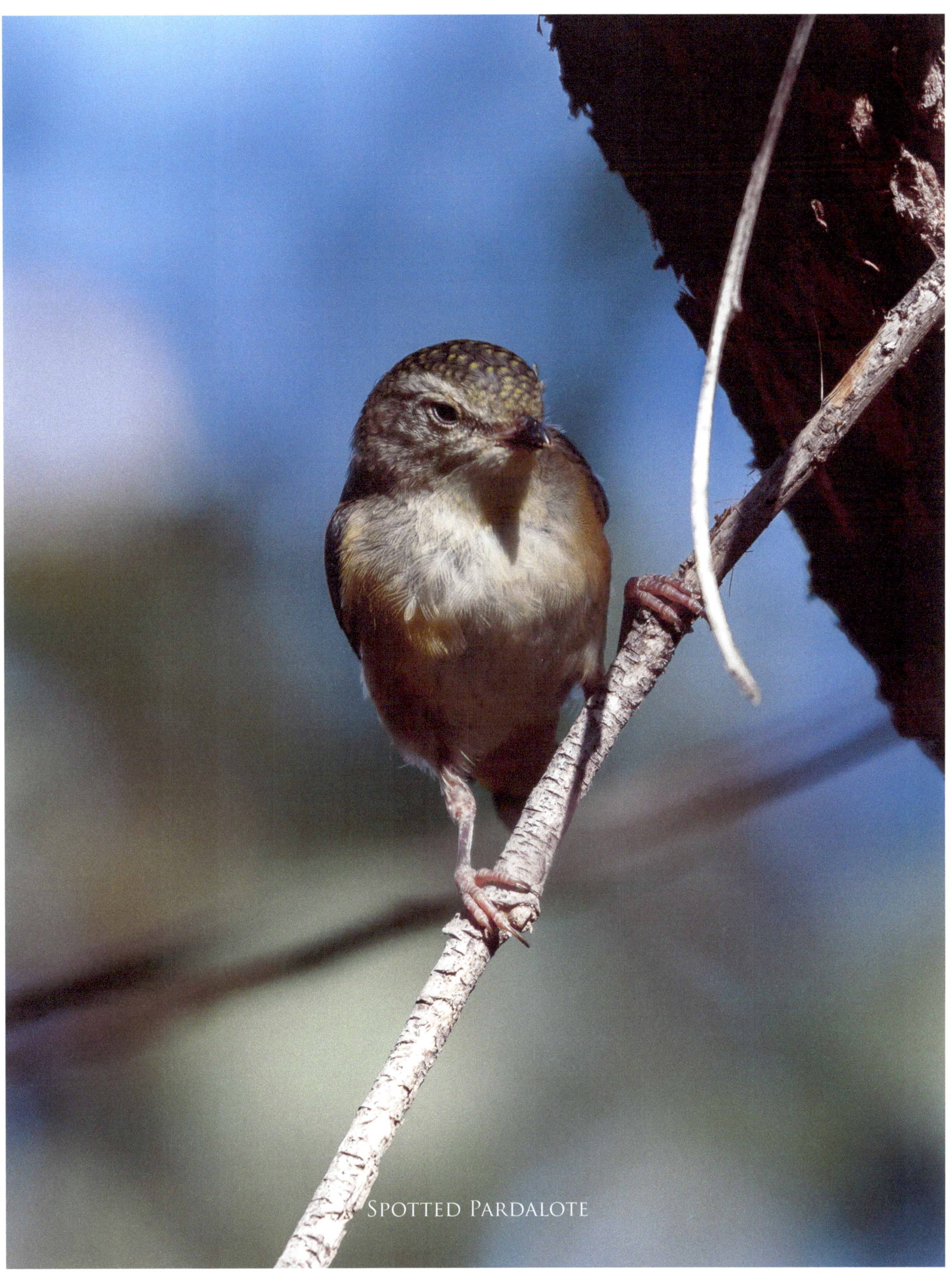

Spotted Pardalote

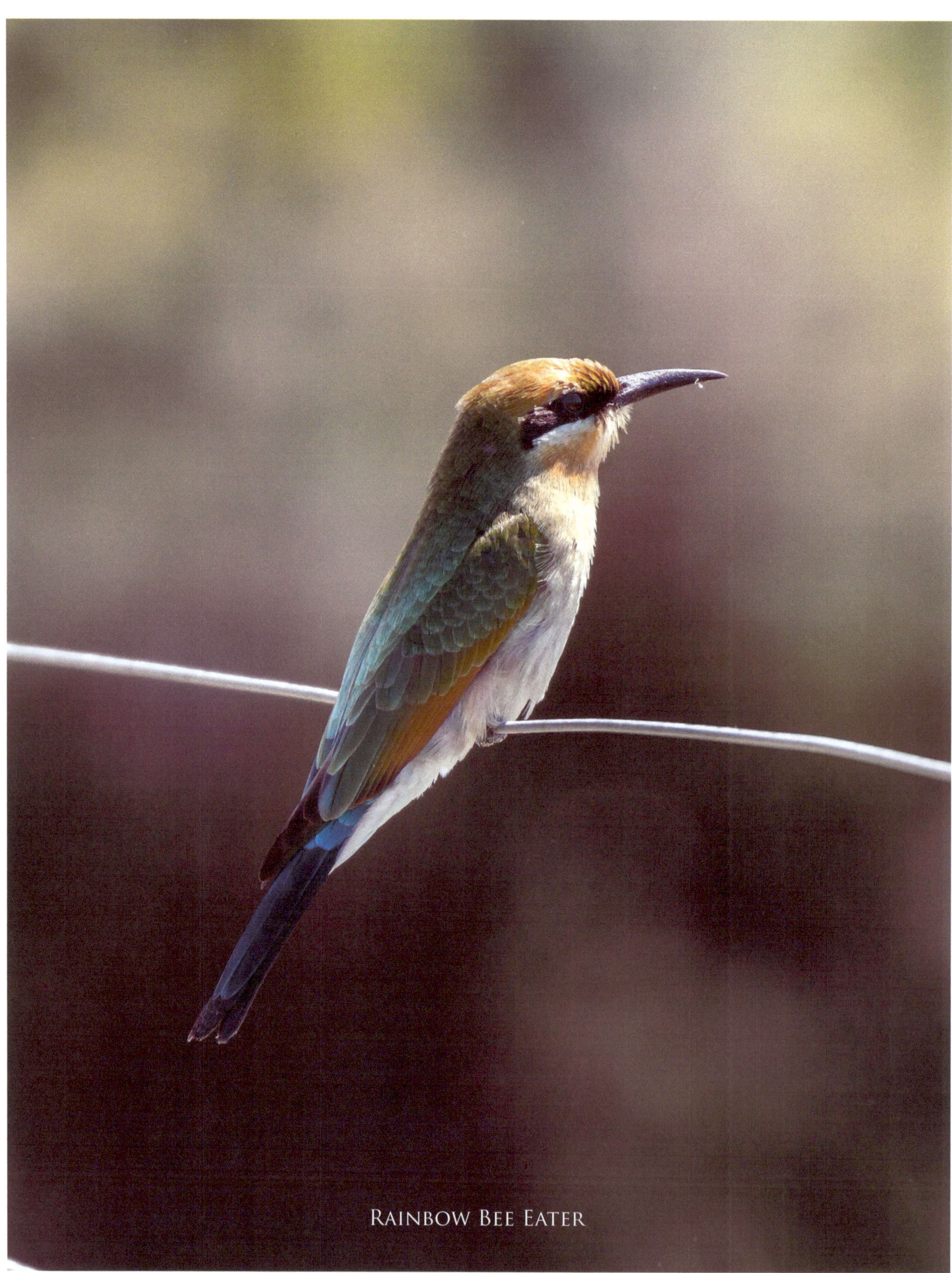

Rainbow Bee Eater

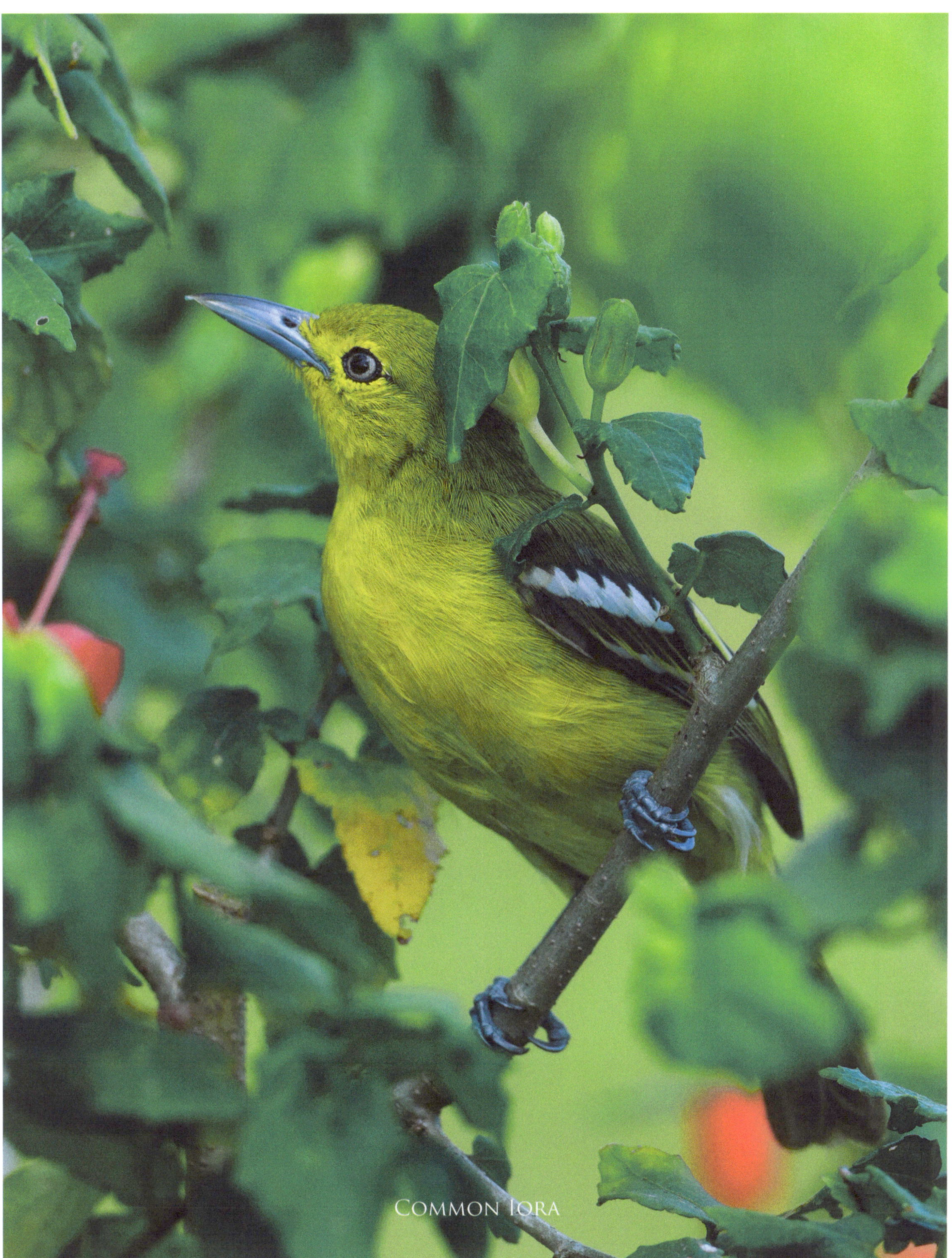

Common Iora

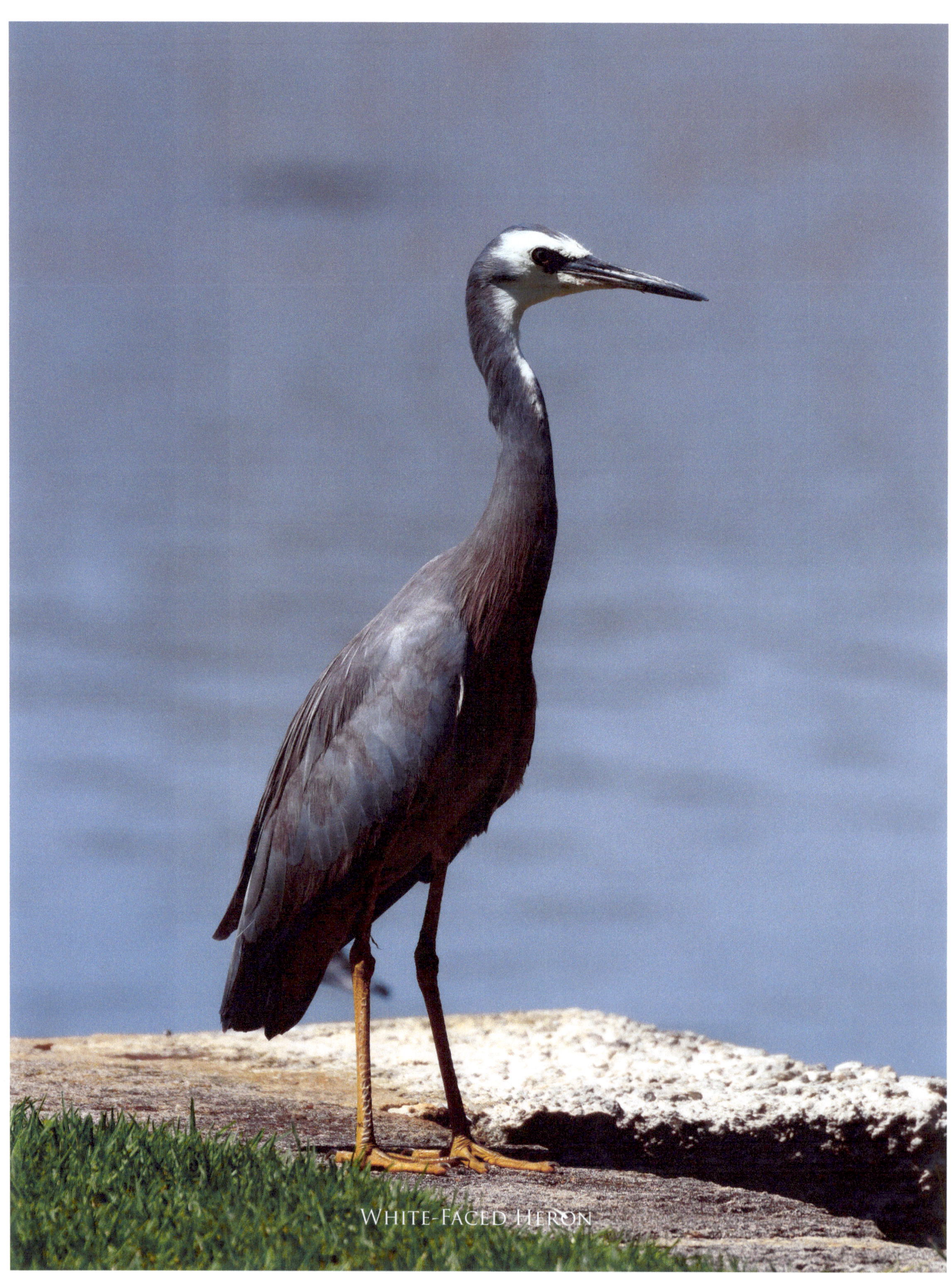

White-Faced Heron

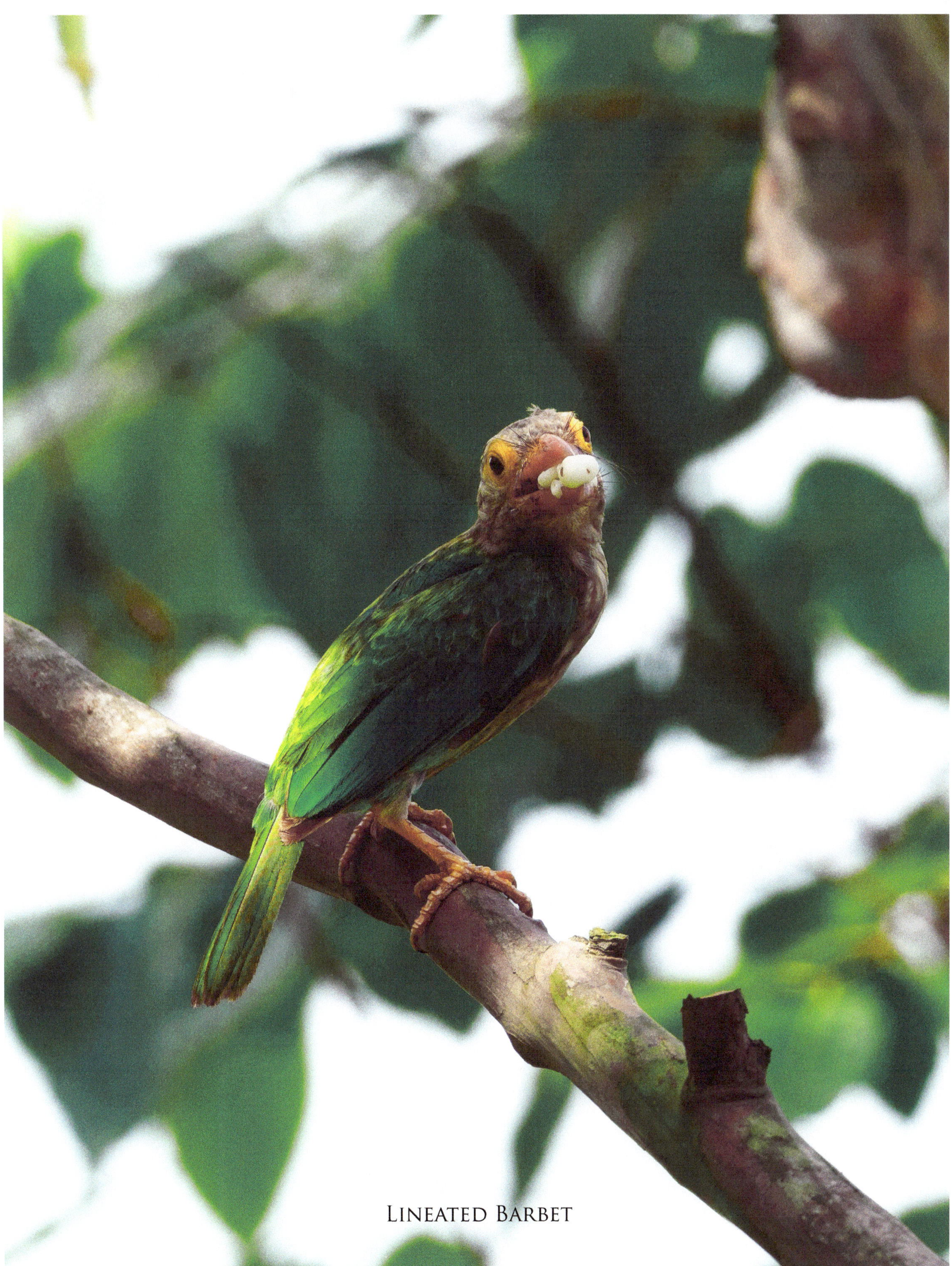

Lineated Barbet

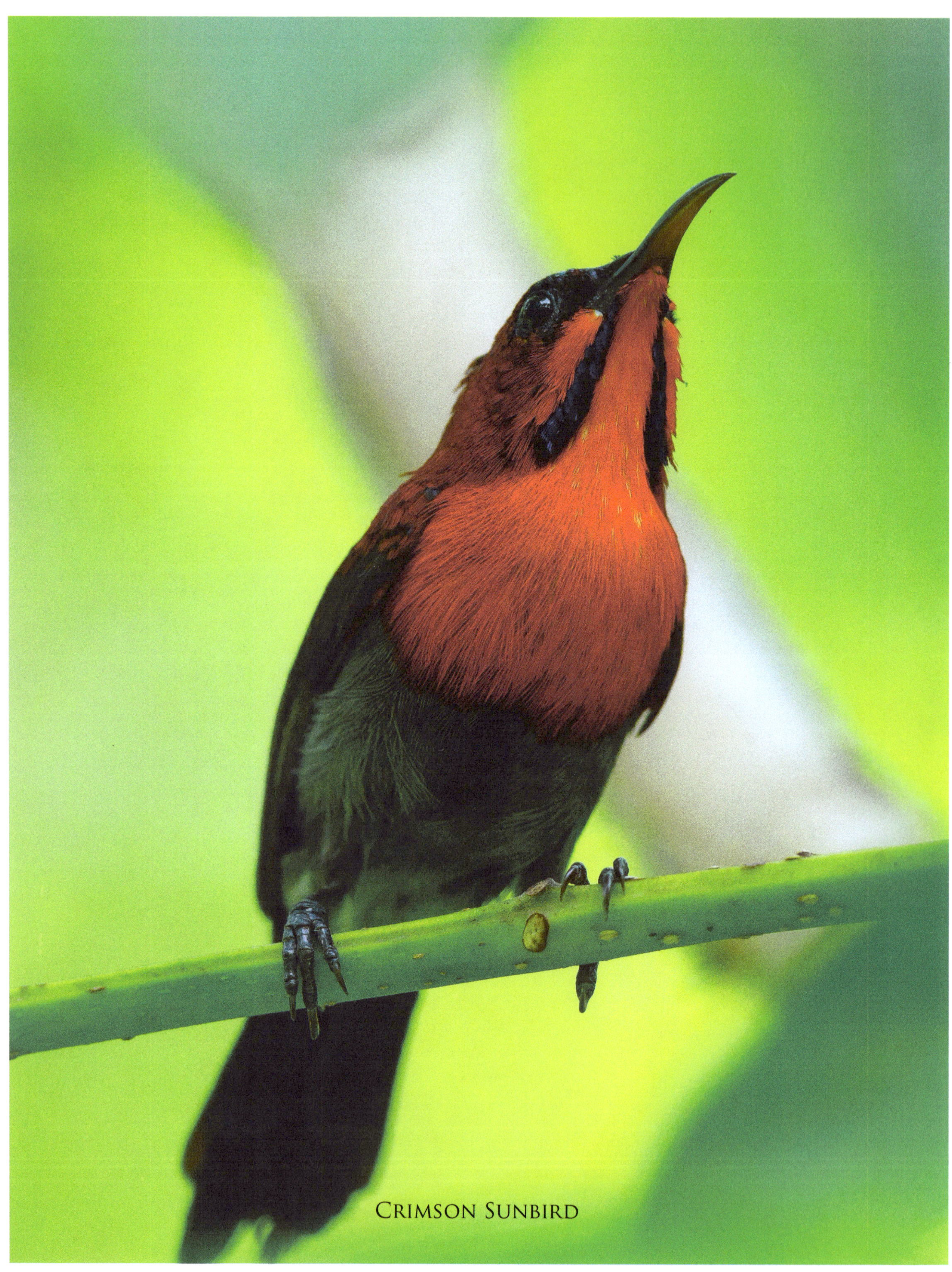

Crimson Sunbird

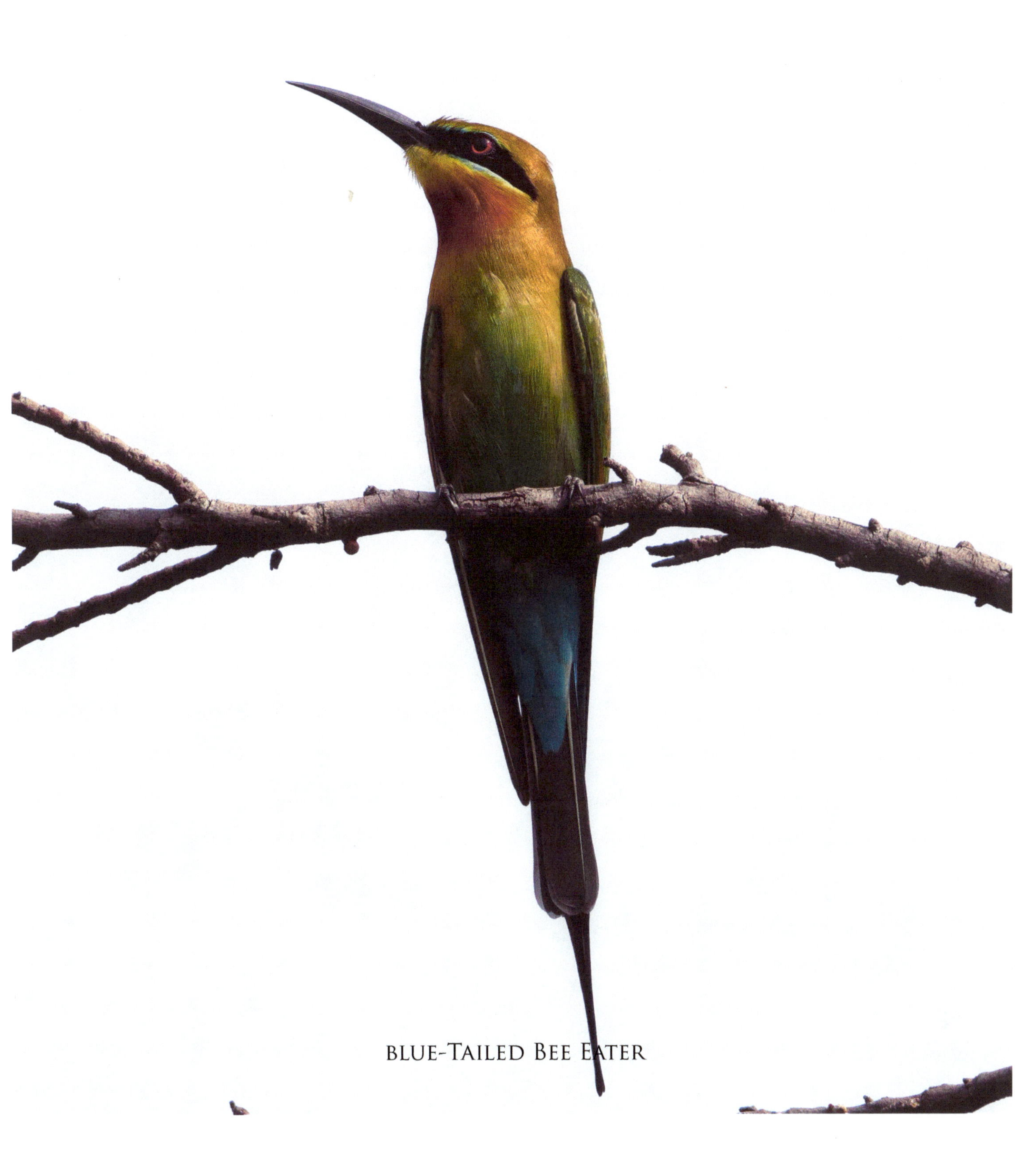

BLUE-TAILED BEE EATER

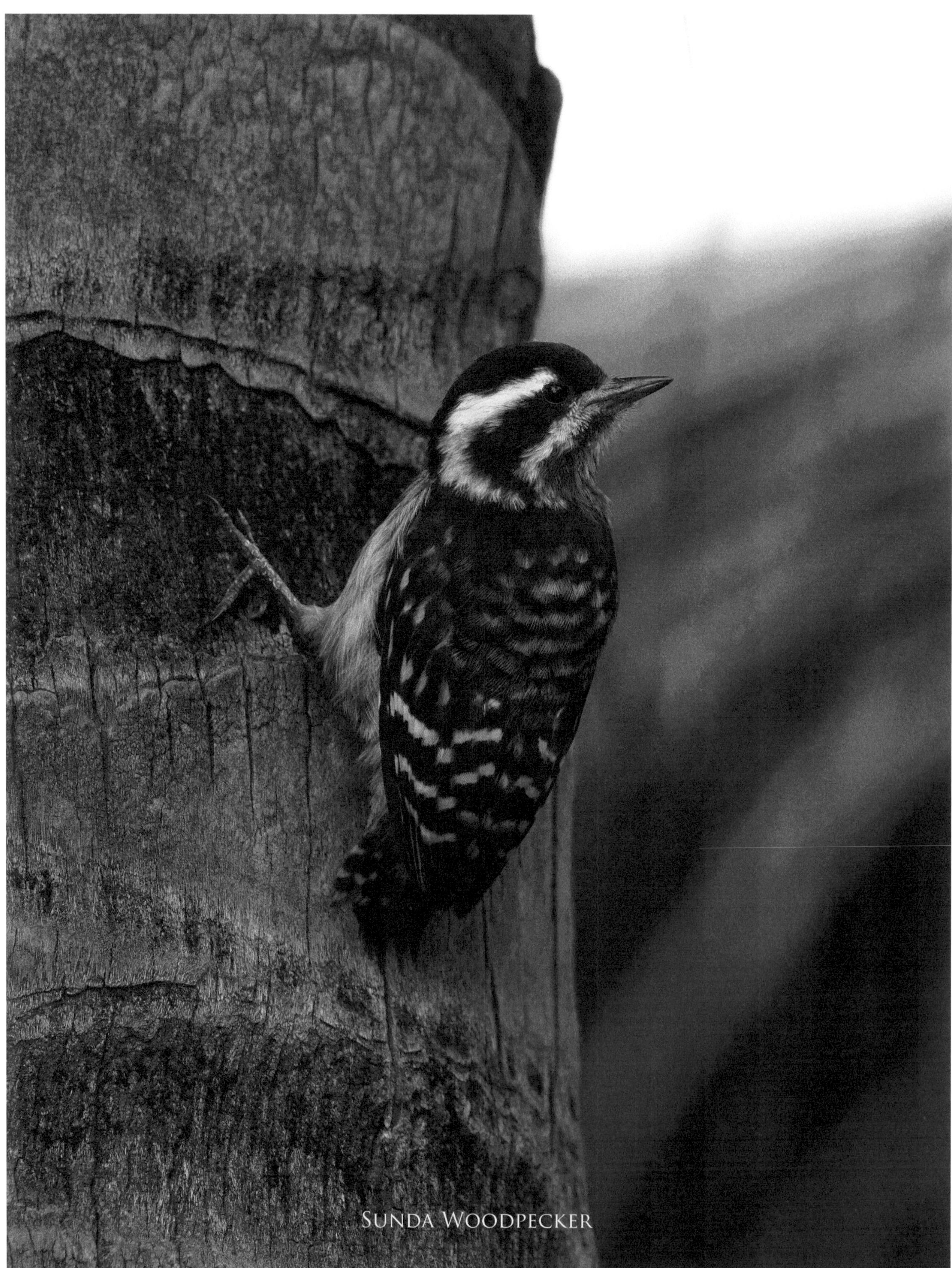

Sunda Woodpecker

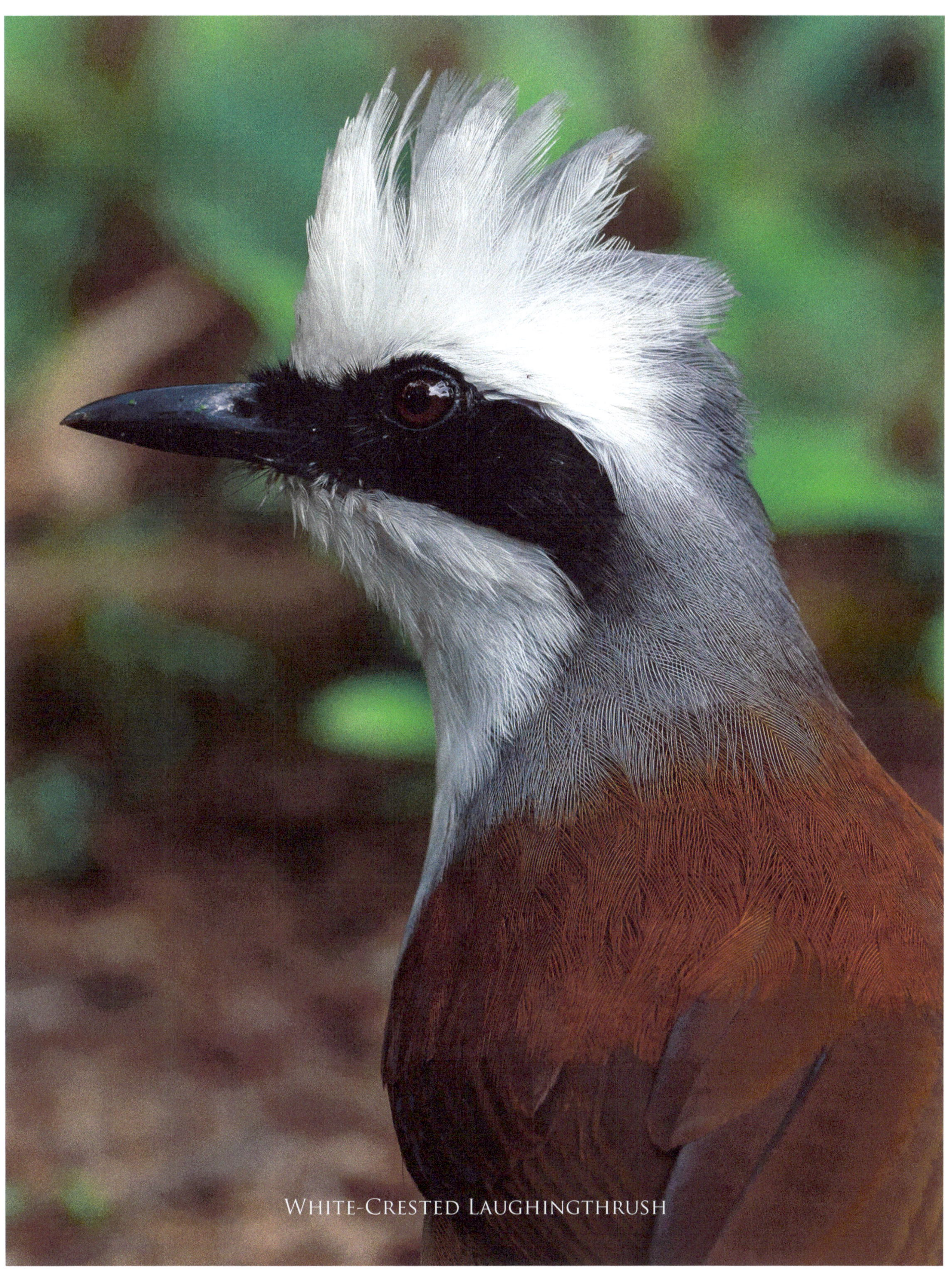

White-Crested Laughingthrush

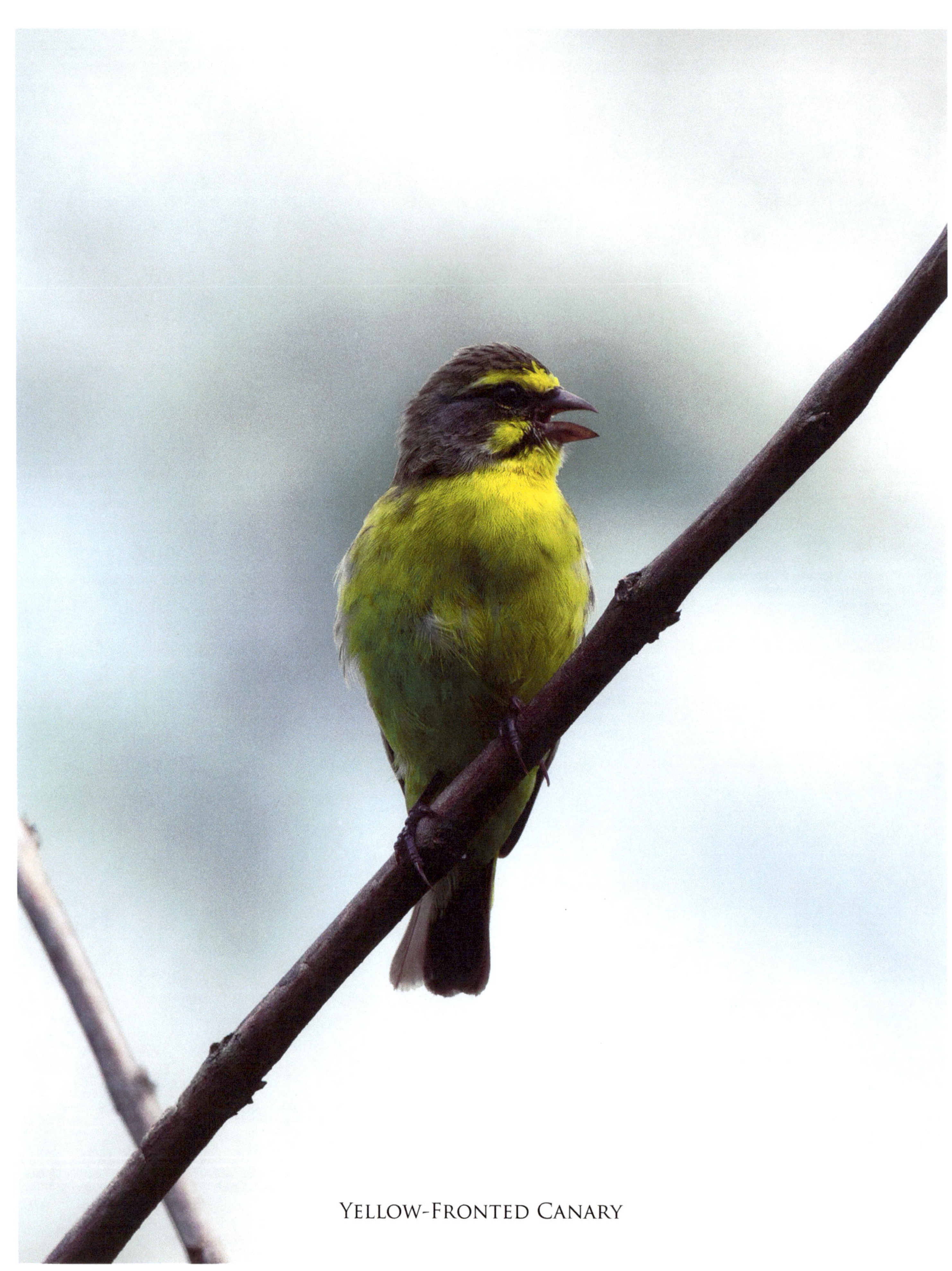

Yellow-Fronted Canary

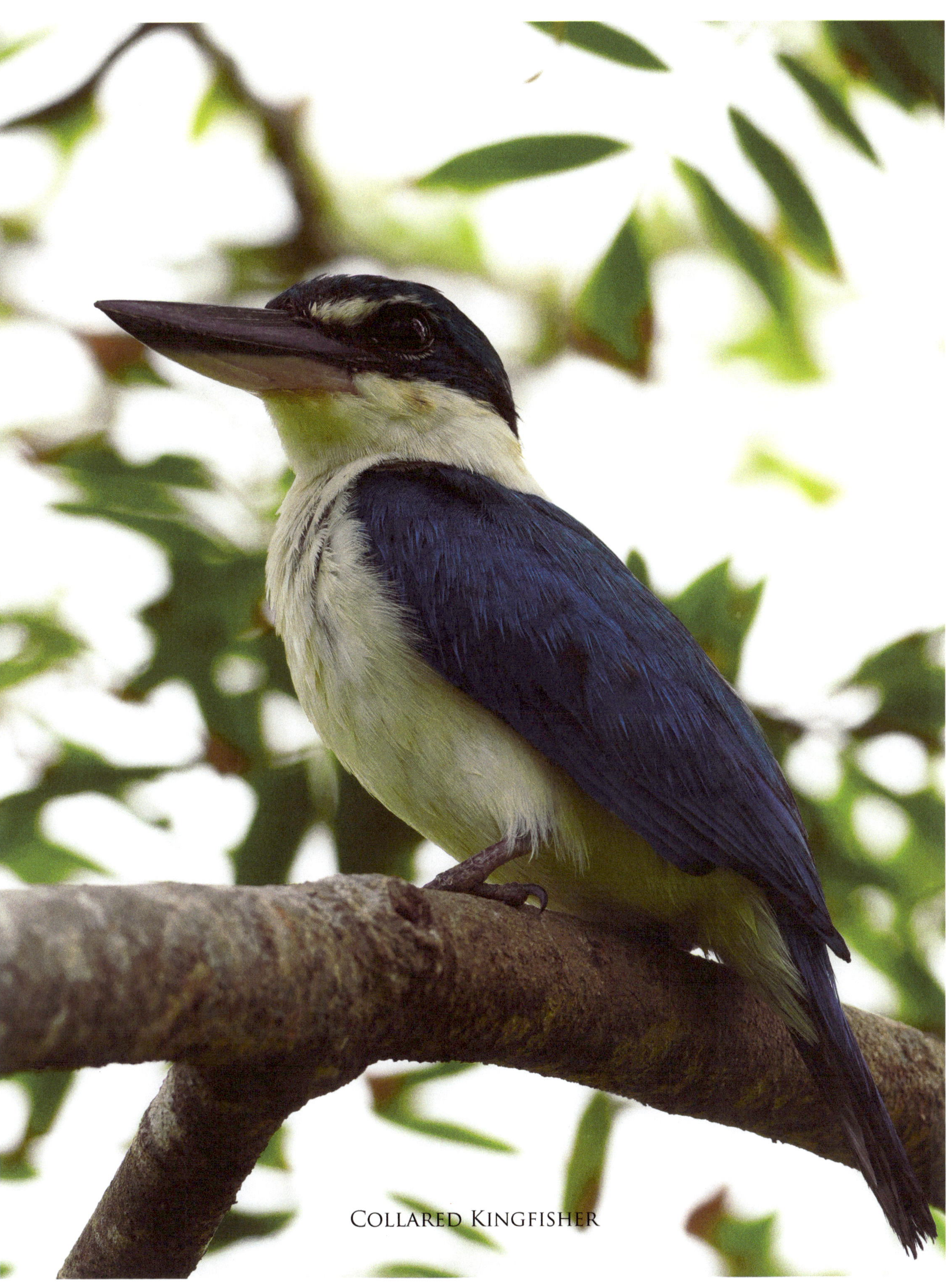

Collared Kingfisher

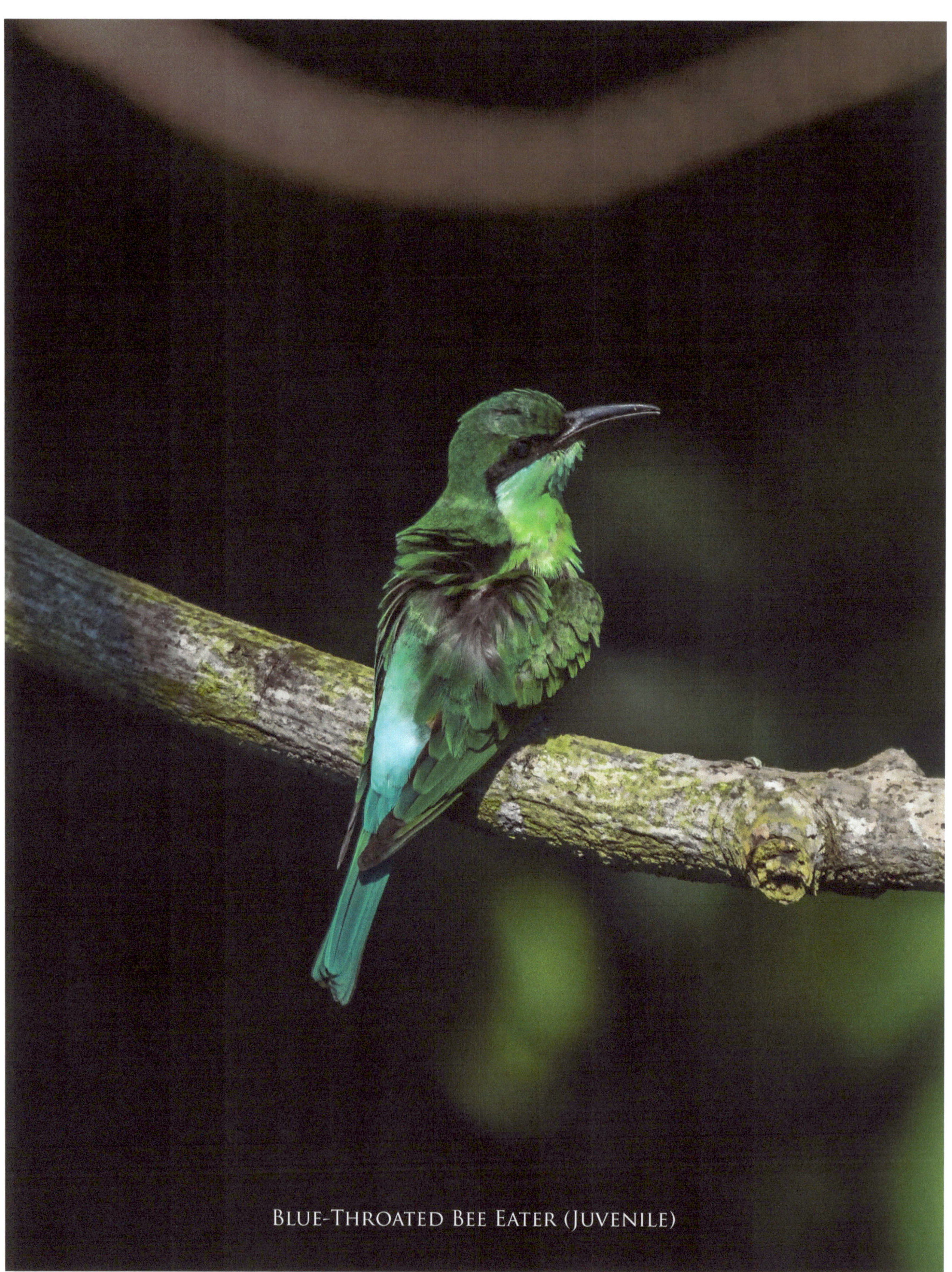

Blue-Throated Bee Eater (Juvenile)

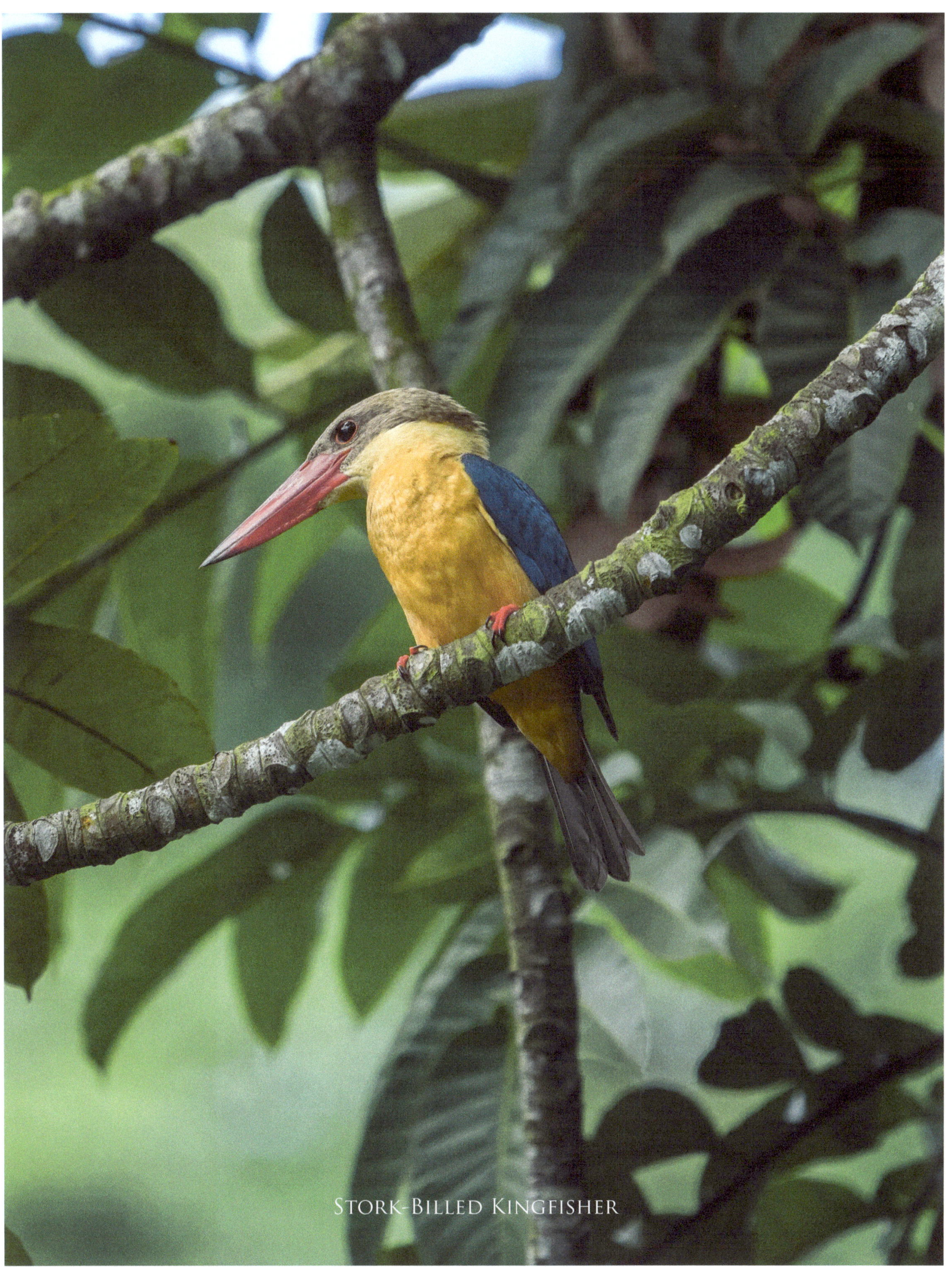

Stork-Billed Kingfisher

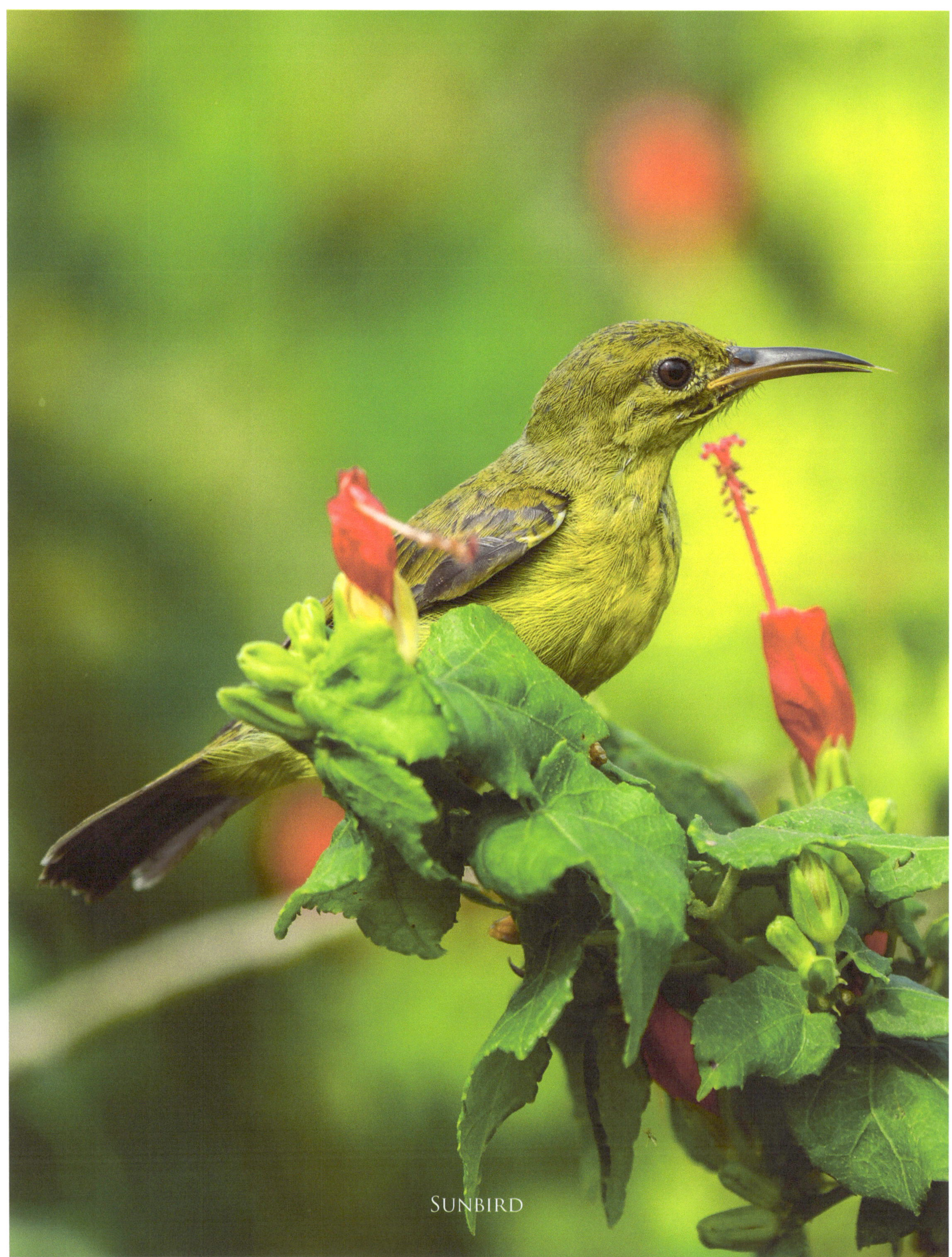

Sunbird

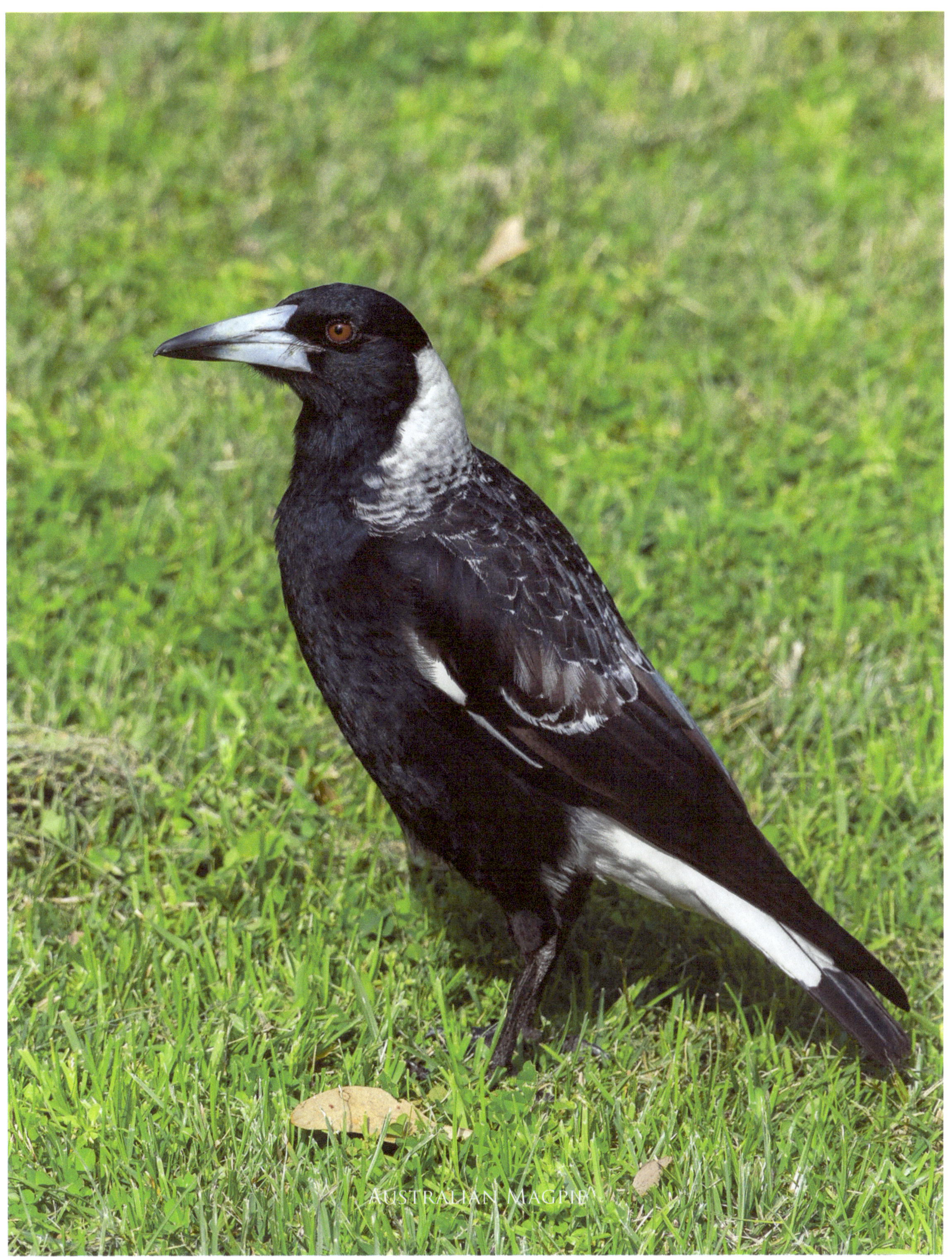

Australian Magpie

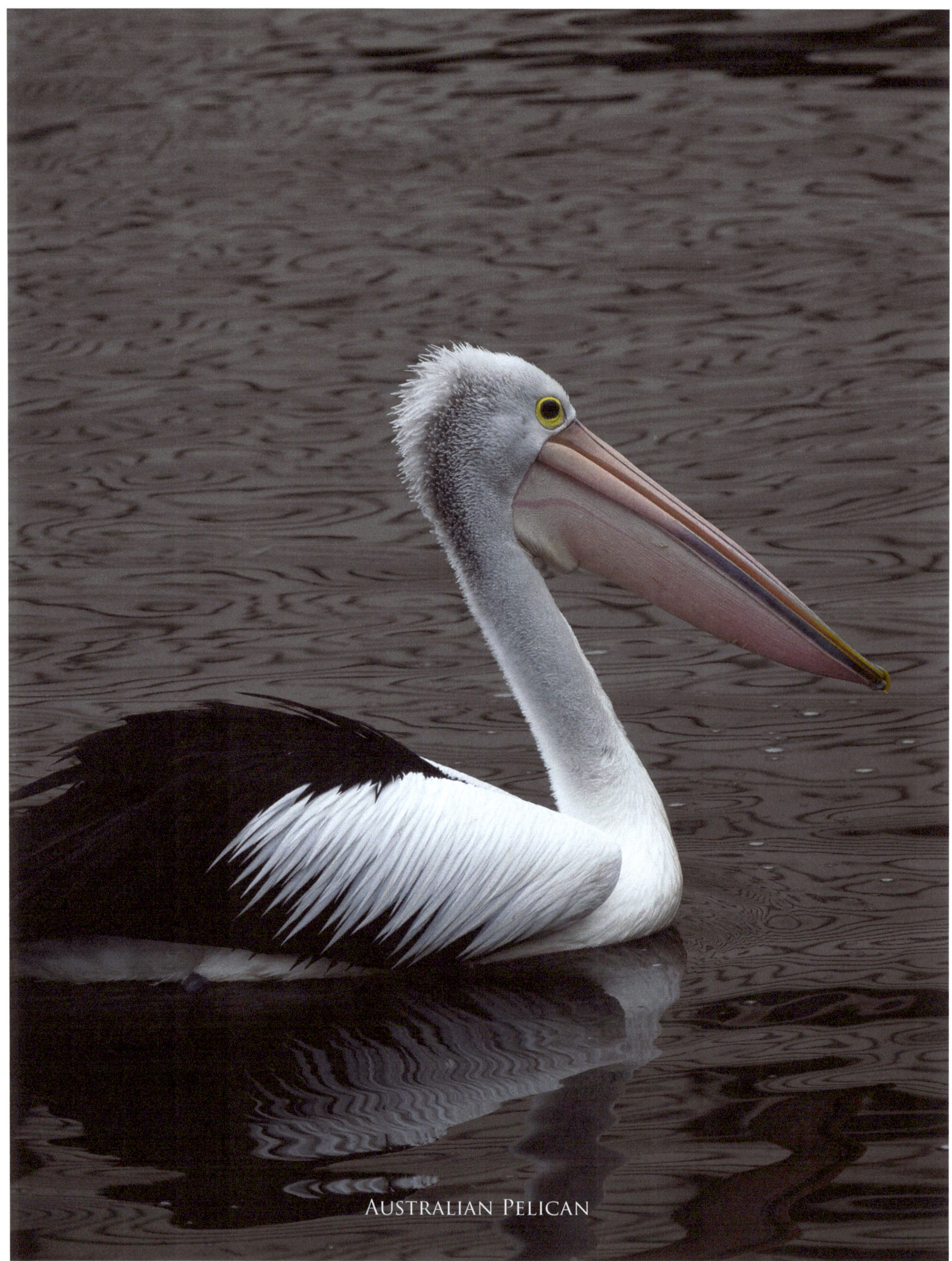

Australian Pelican

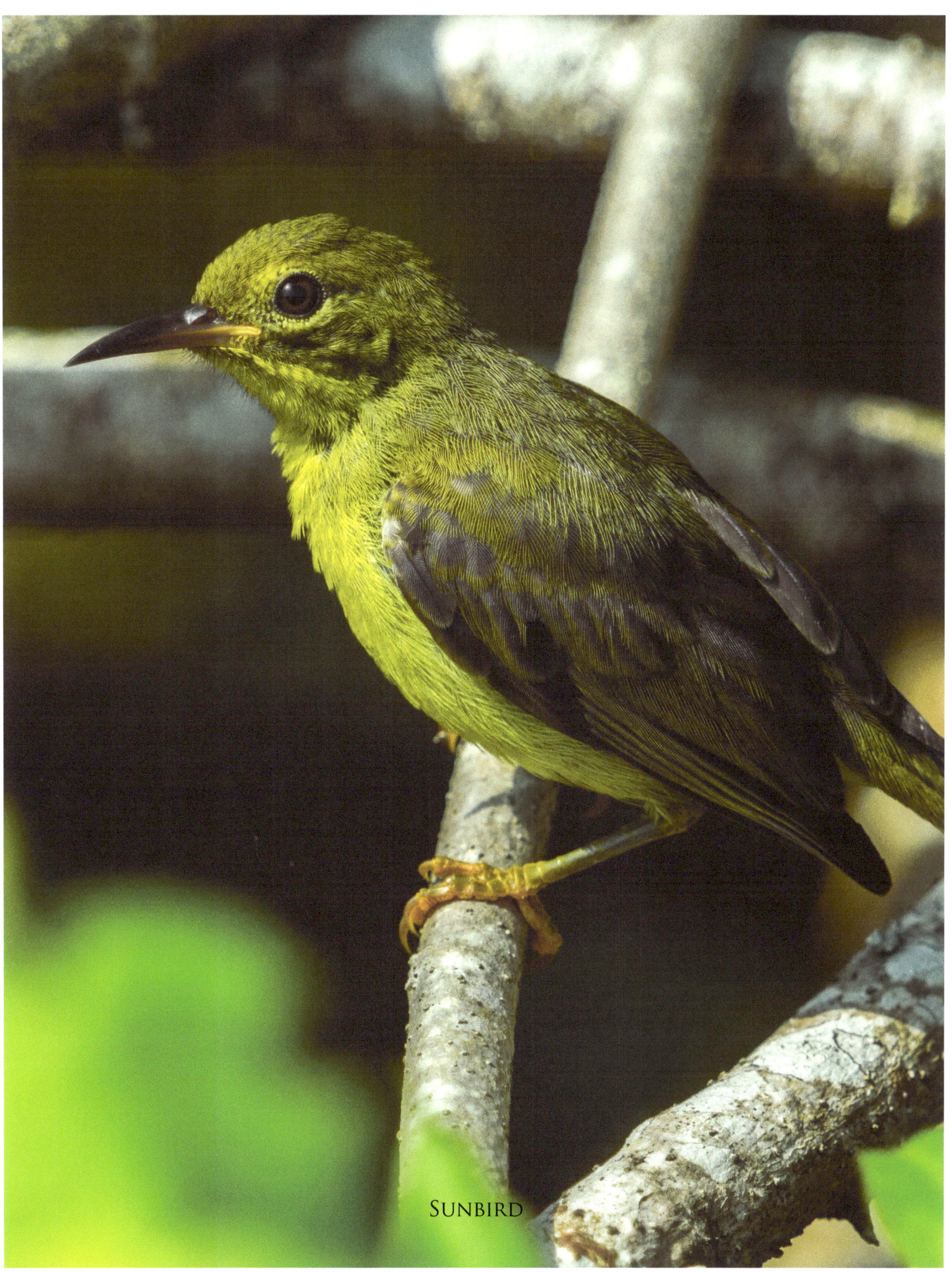

Sunbird

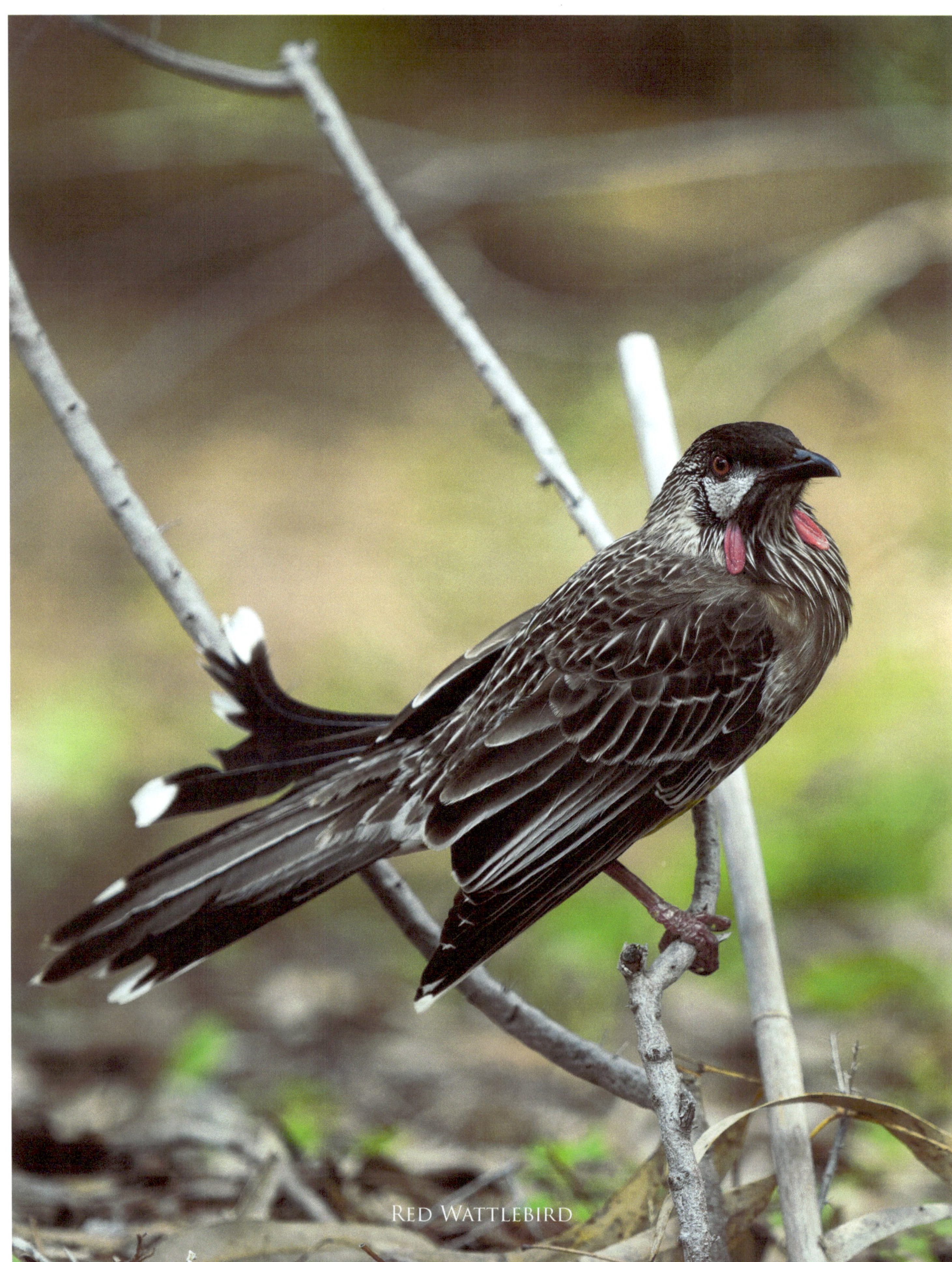

Red Wattlebird

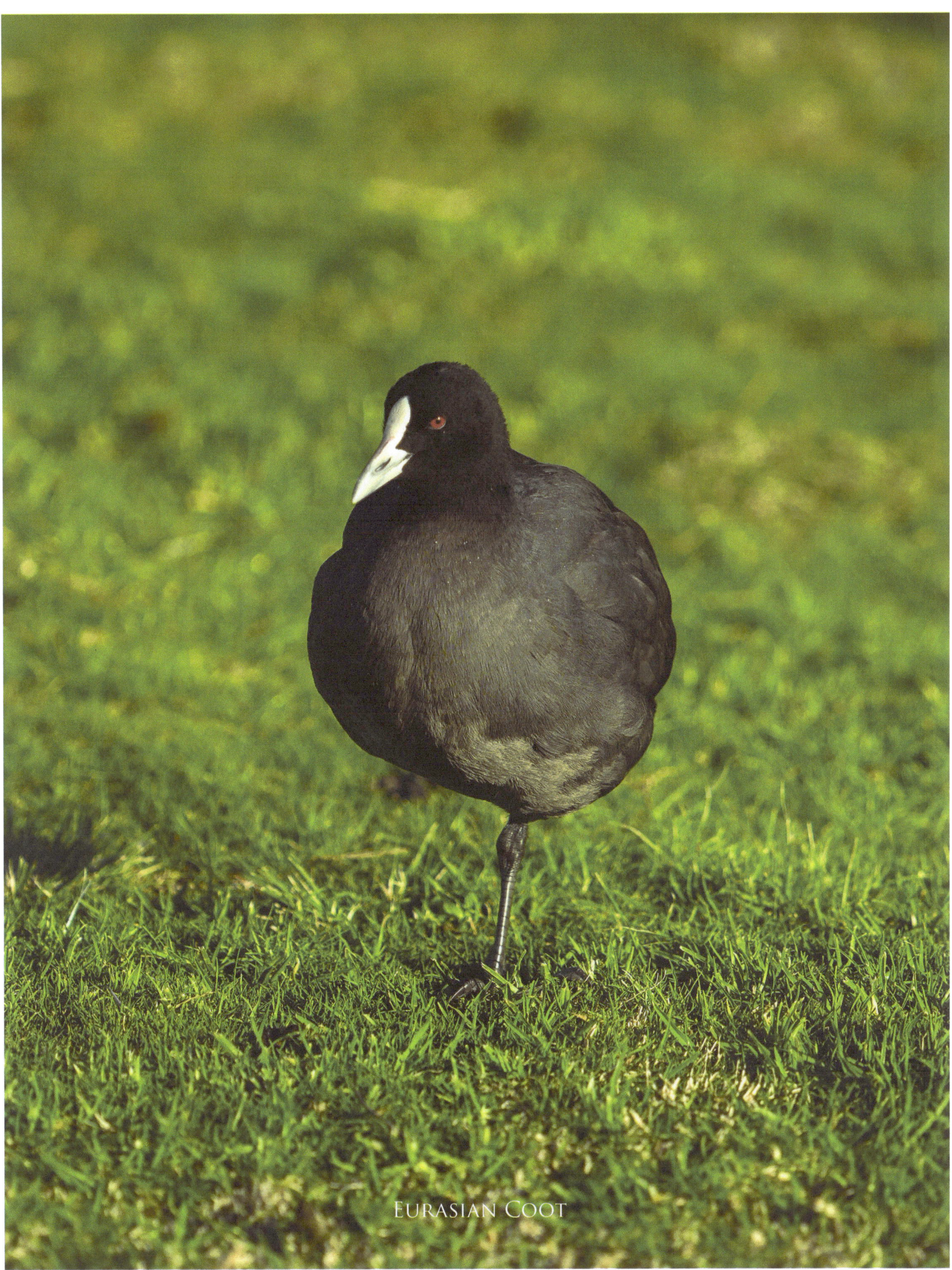

Eurasian Coot

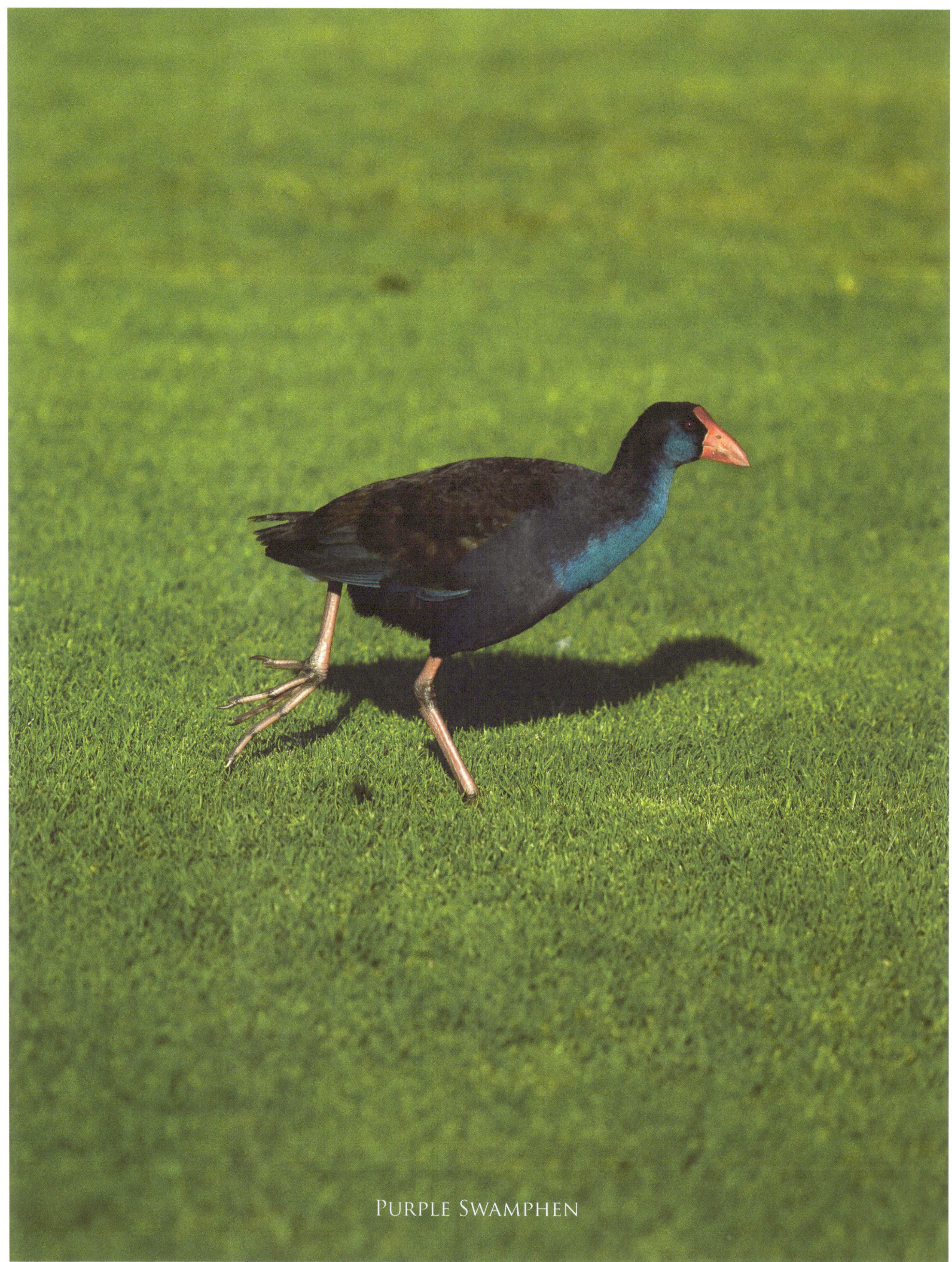

Purple Swamphen

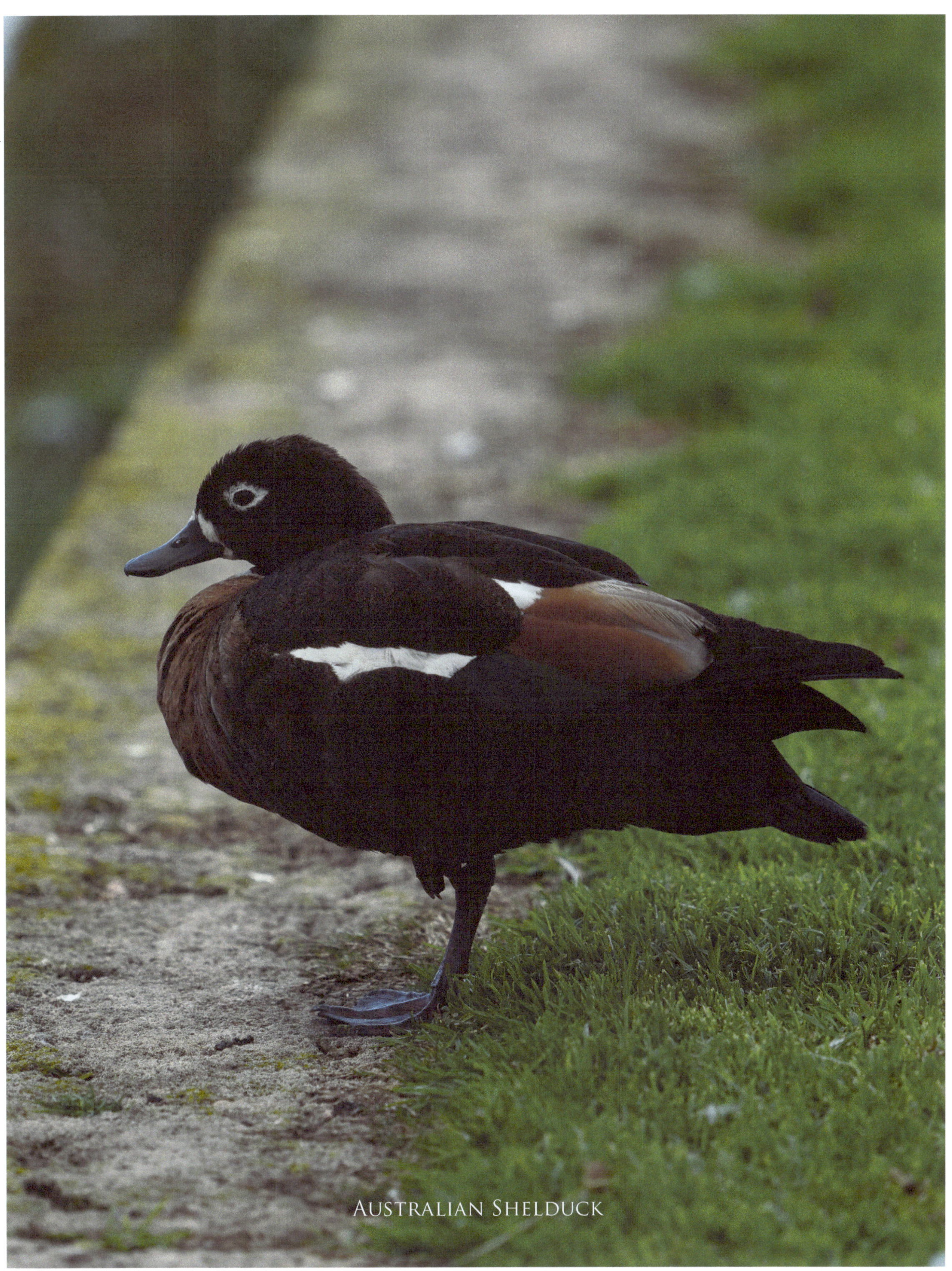

Australian Shelduck

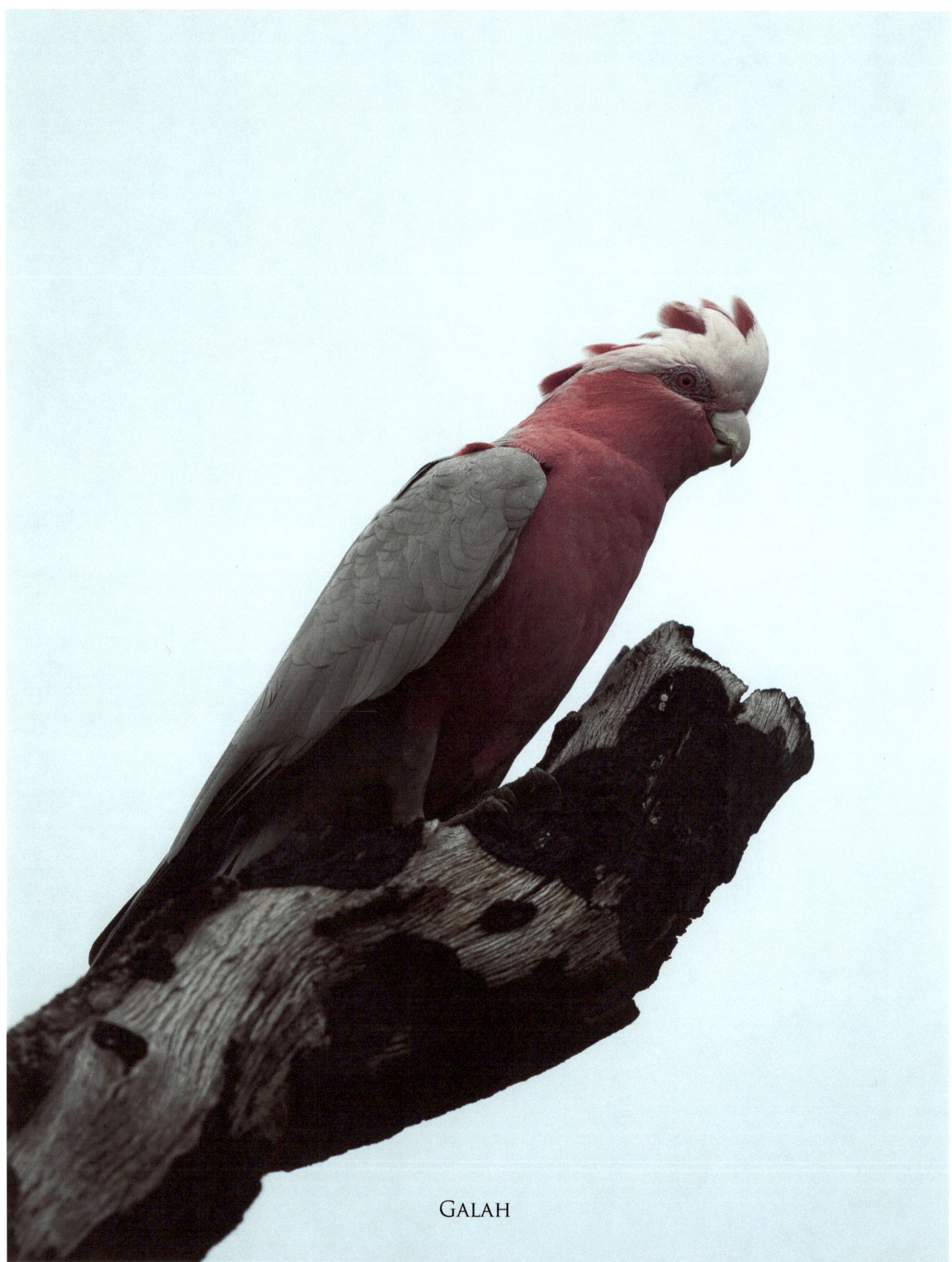

GALAH

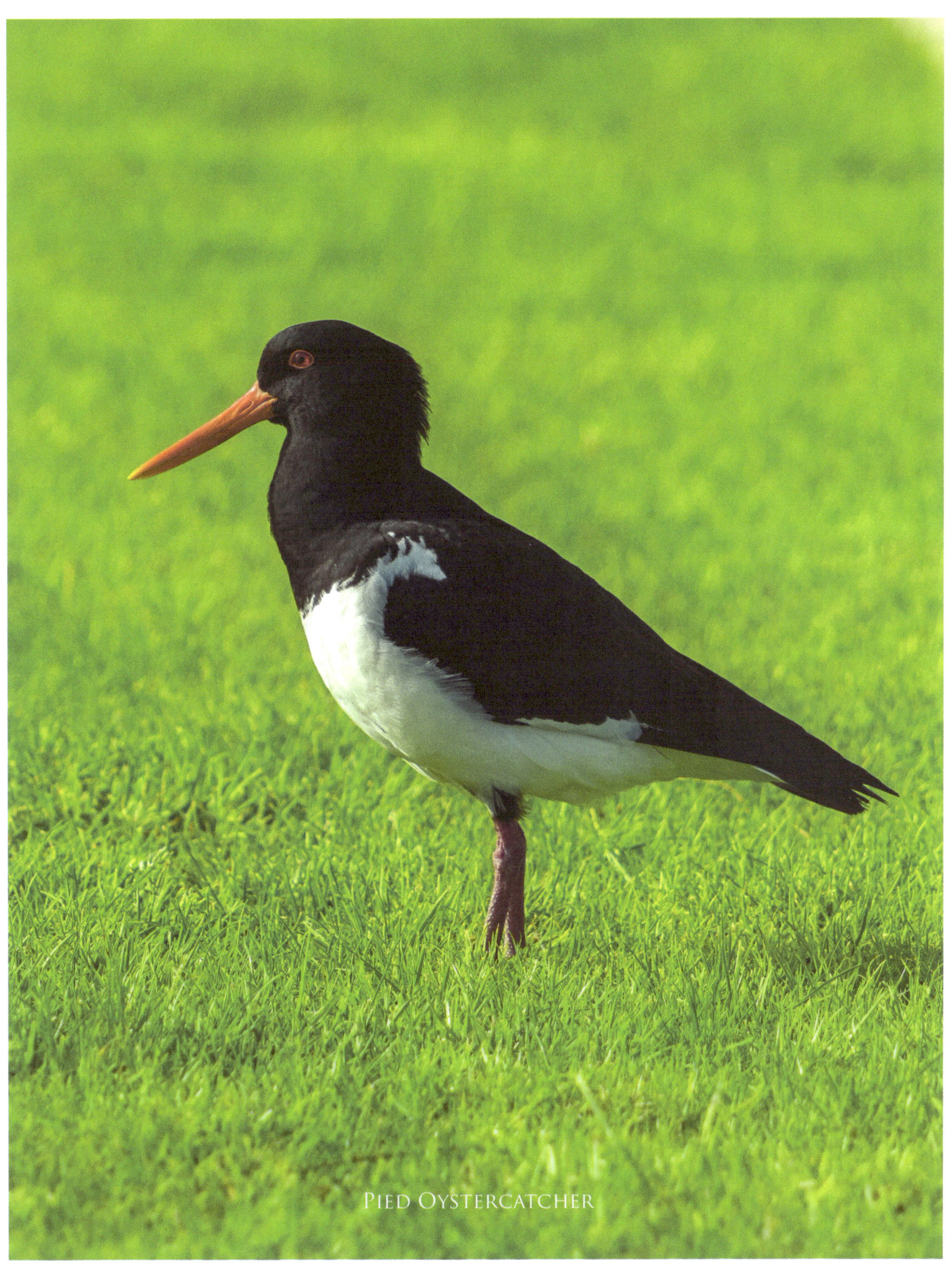

Pied Oystercatcher

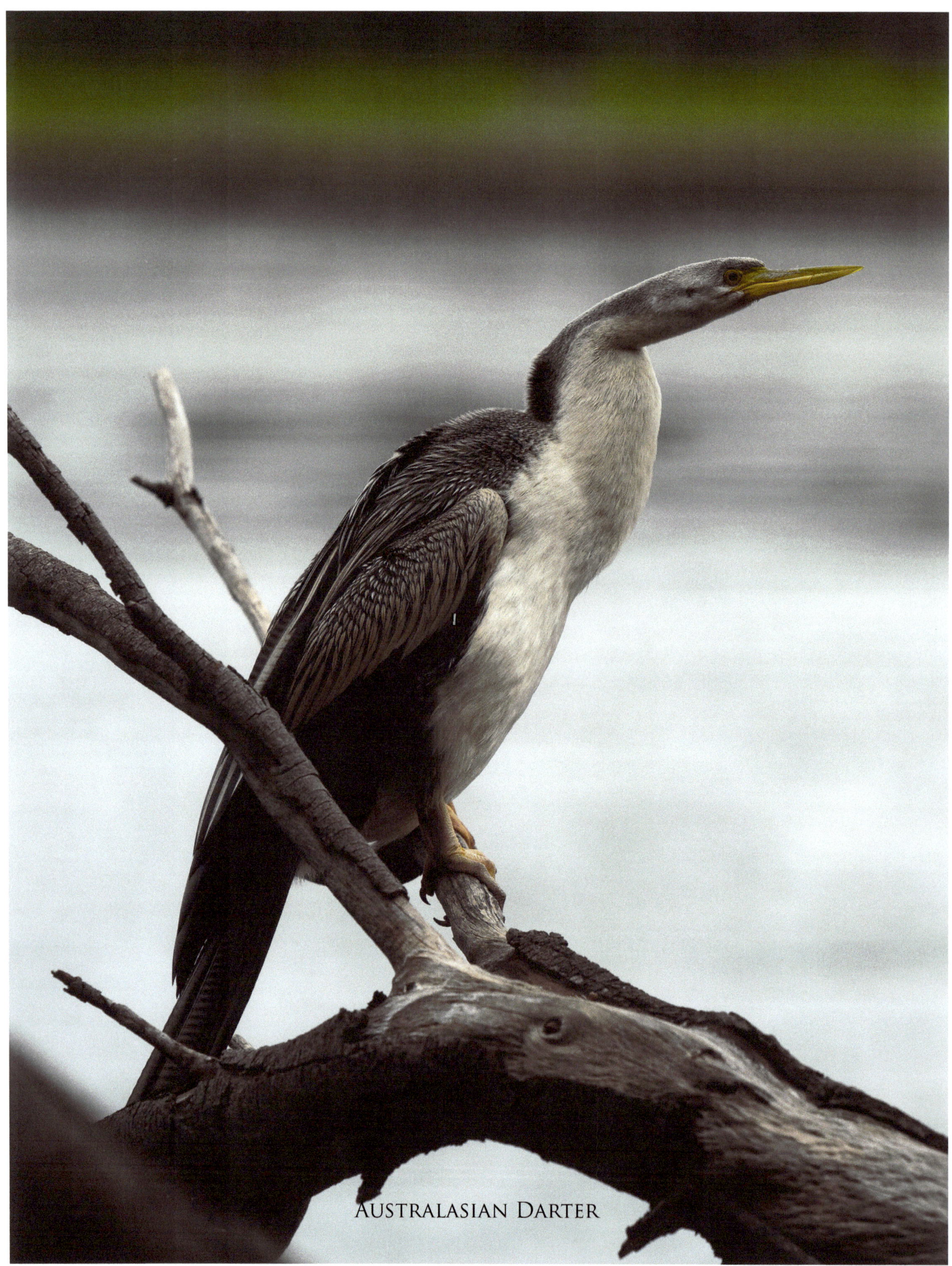

Australasian Darter

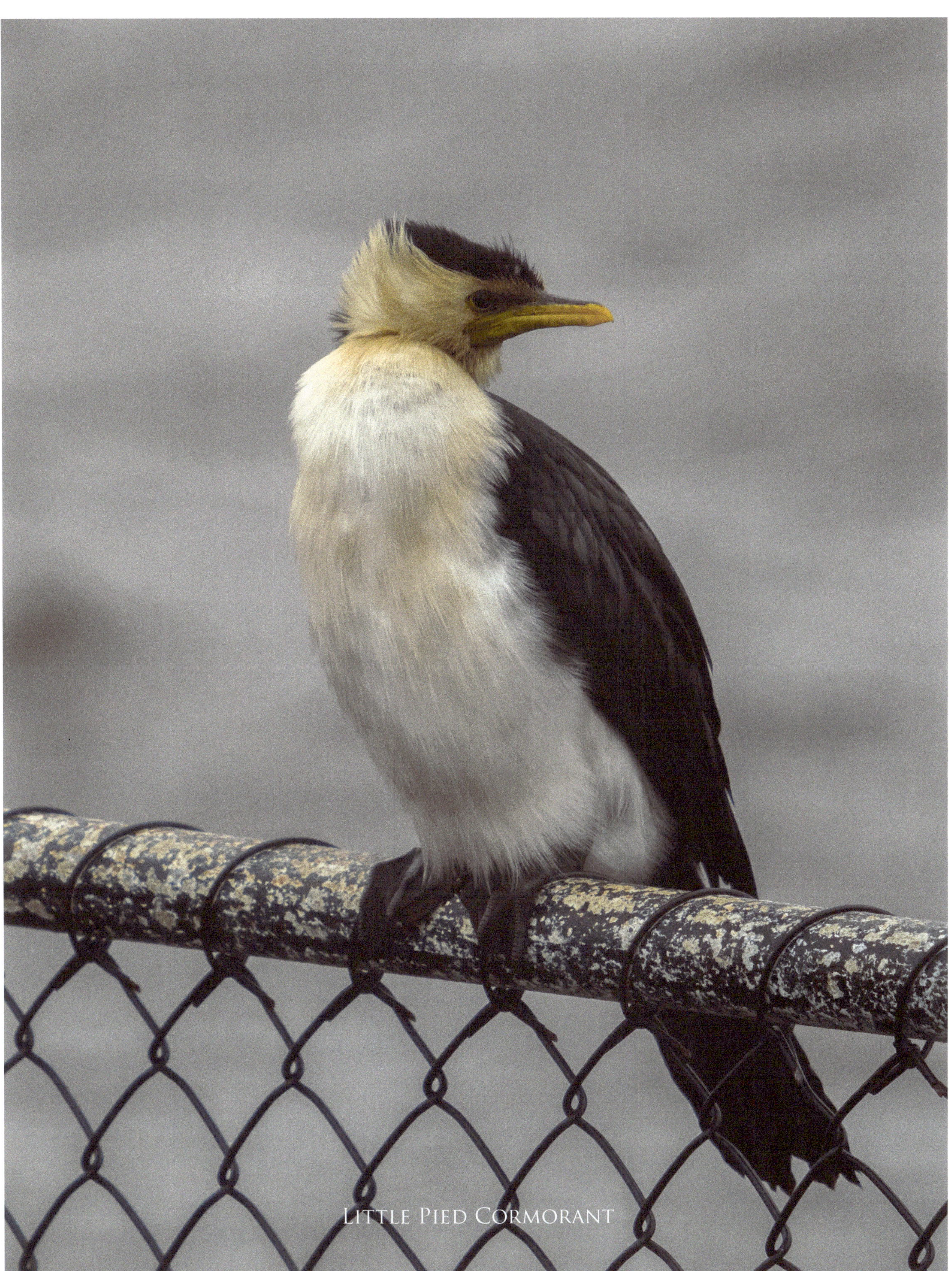
Little Pied Cormorant

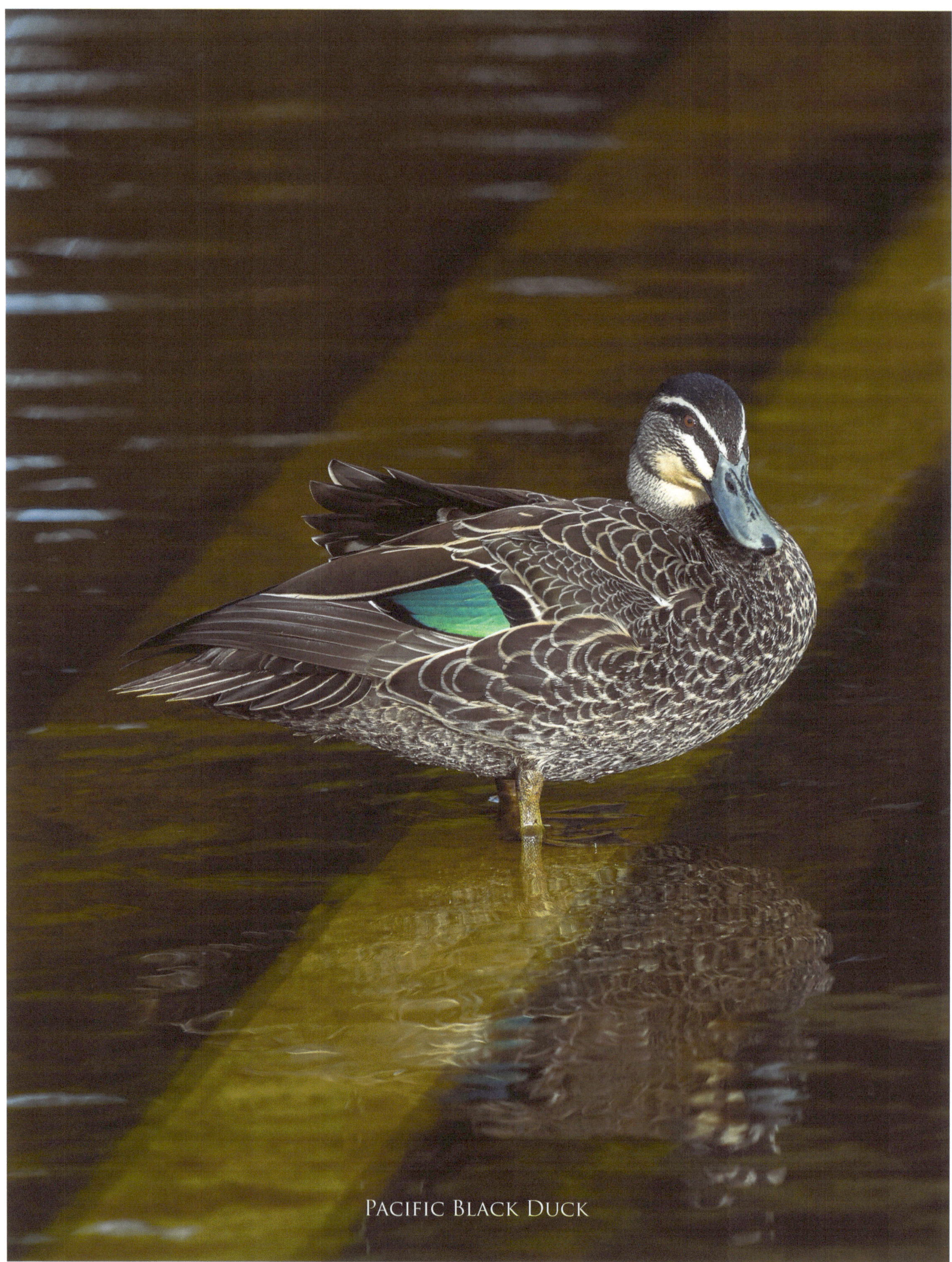

Pacific Black Duck

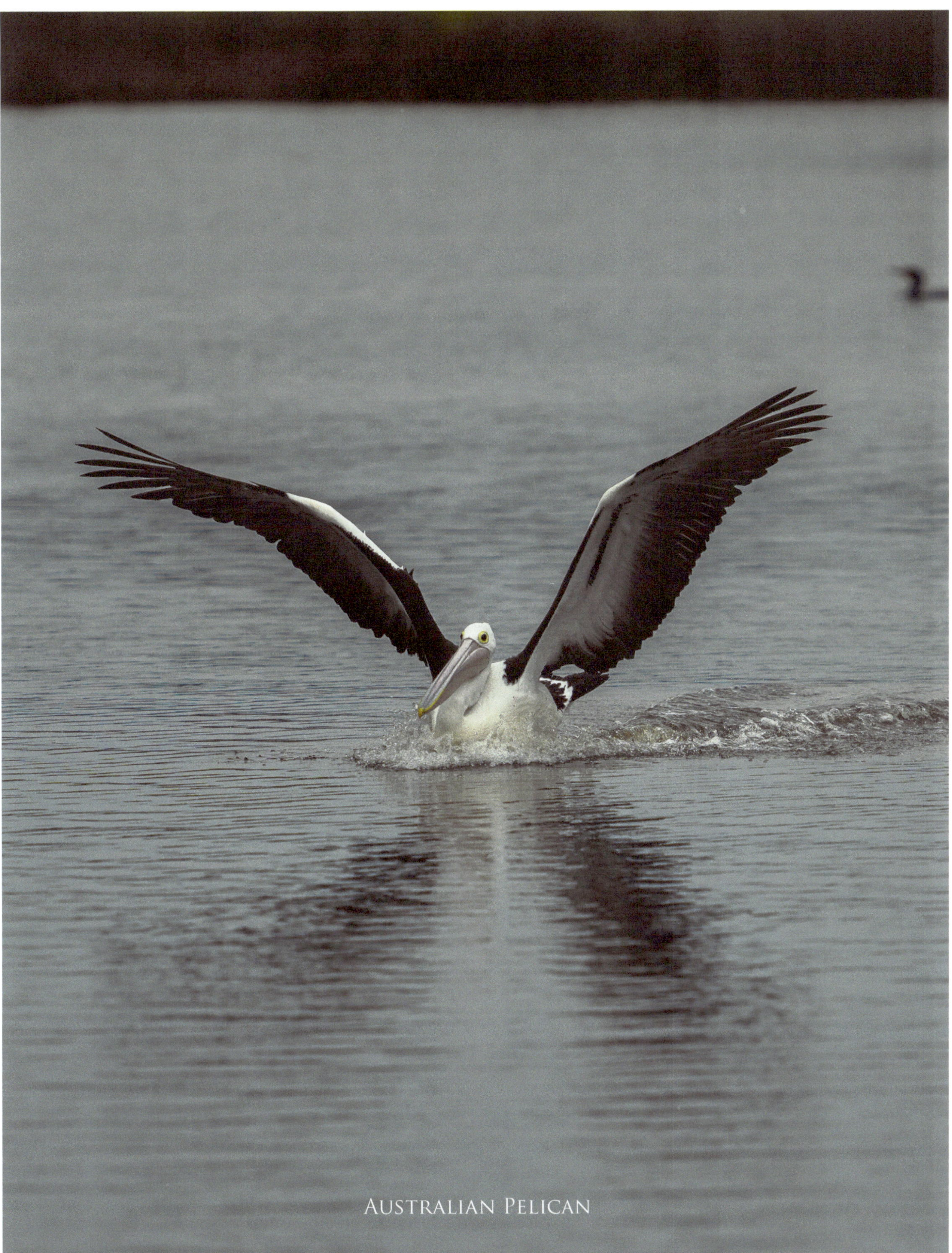

Australian Pelican

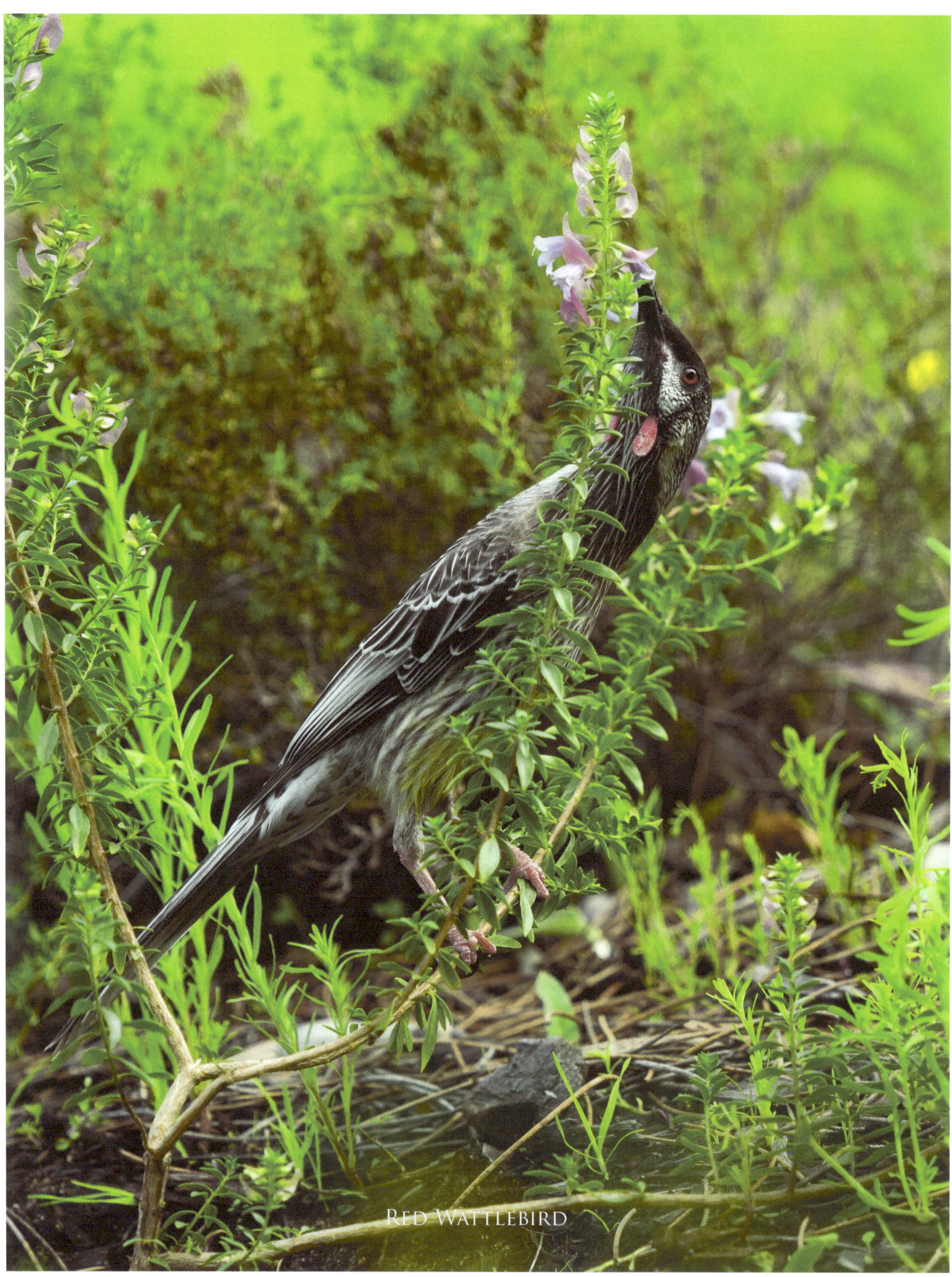
Red Wattlebird

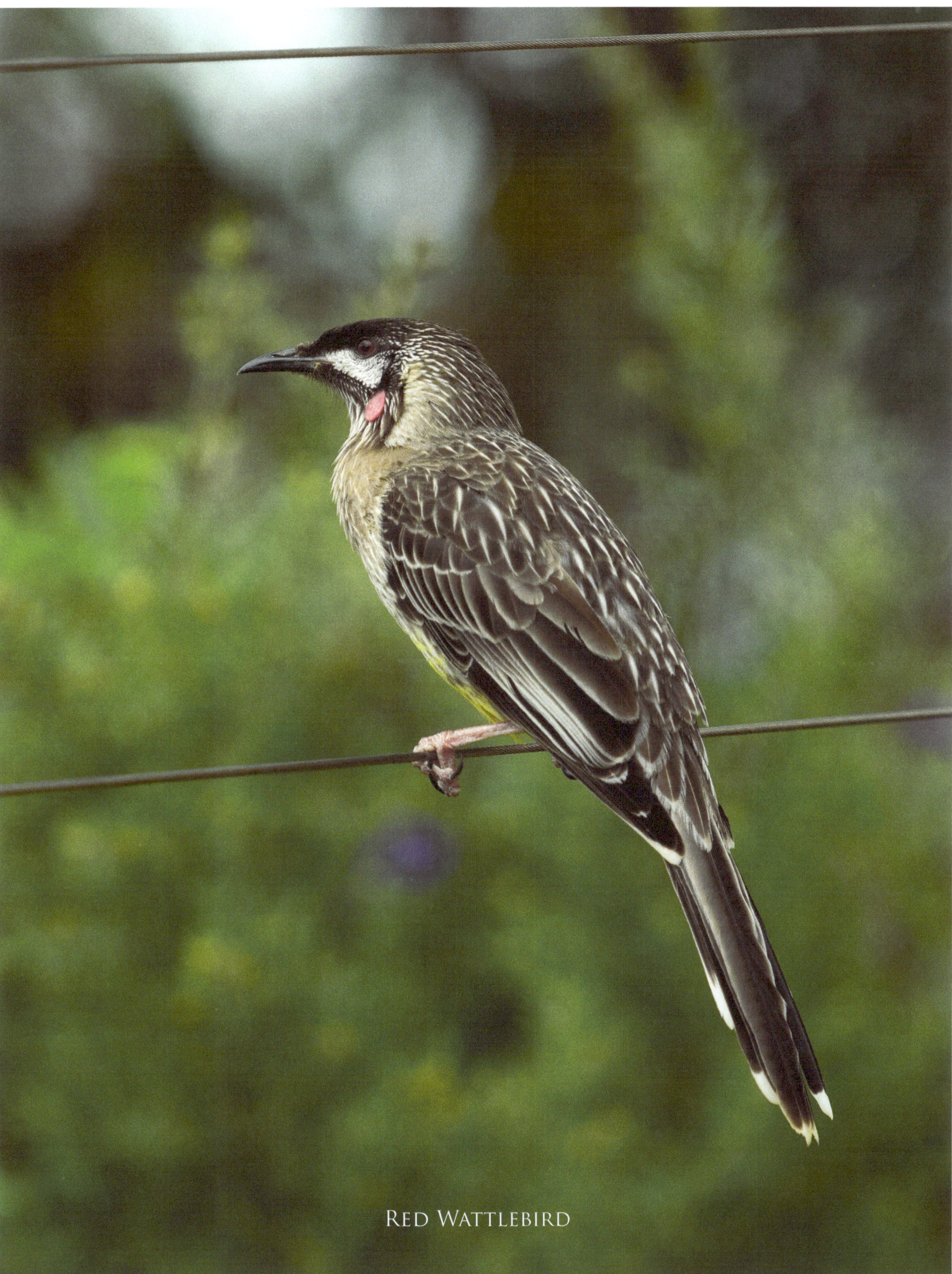

Red Wattlebird

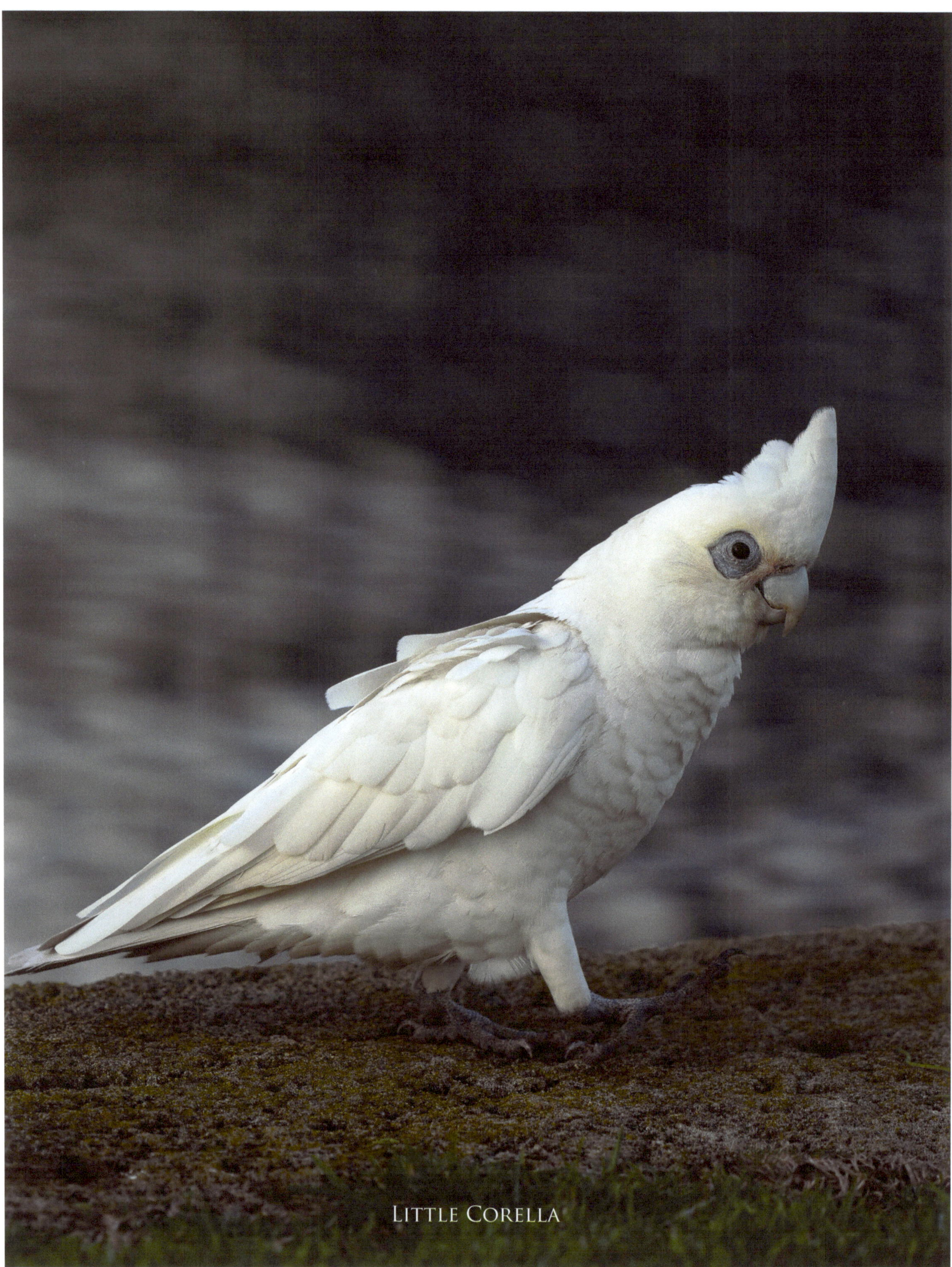

Little Corella

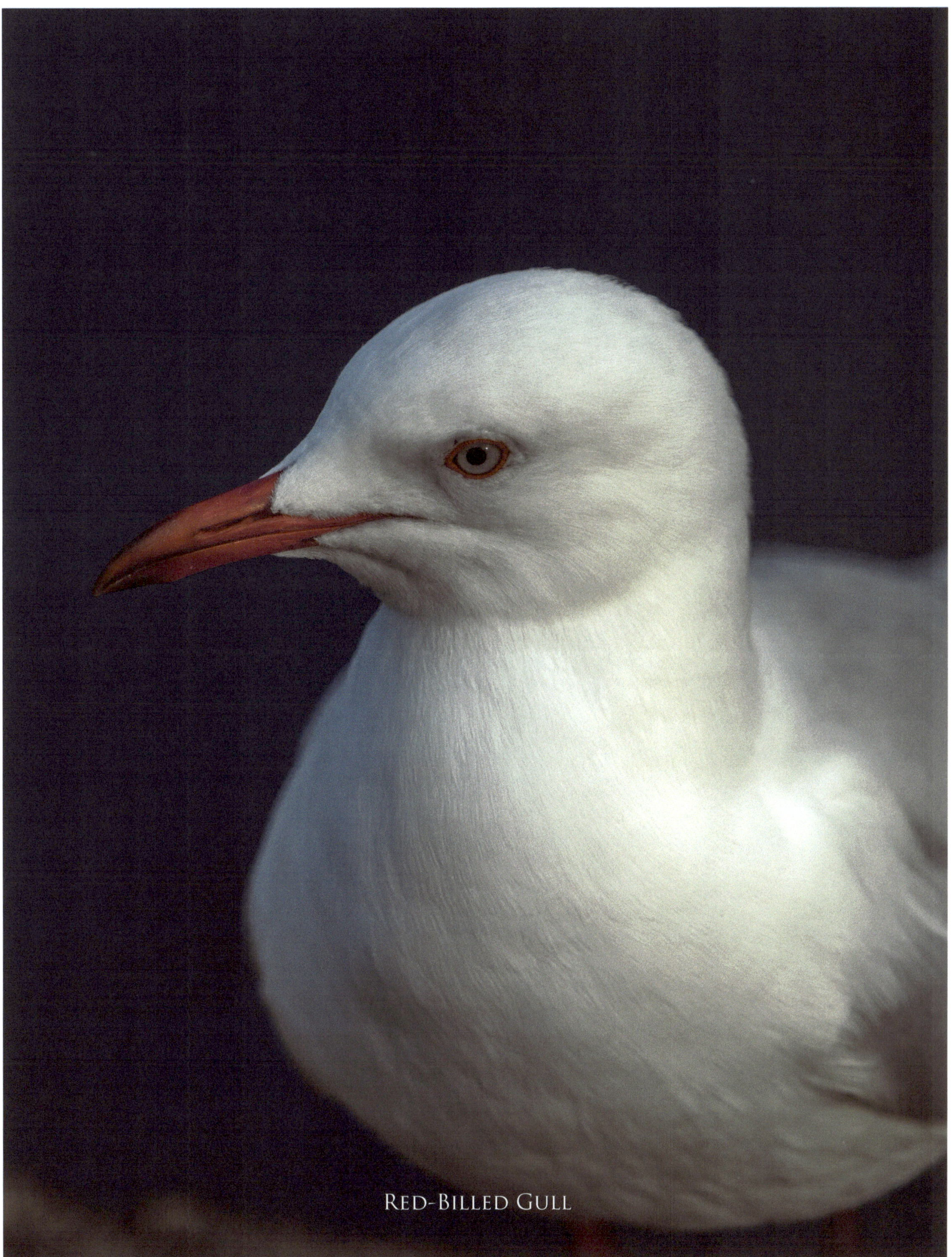
Red-Billed Gull

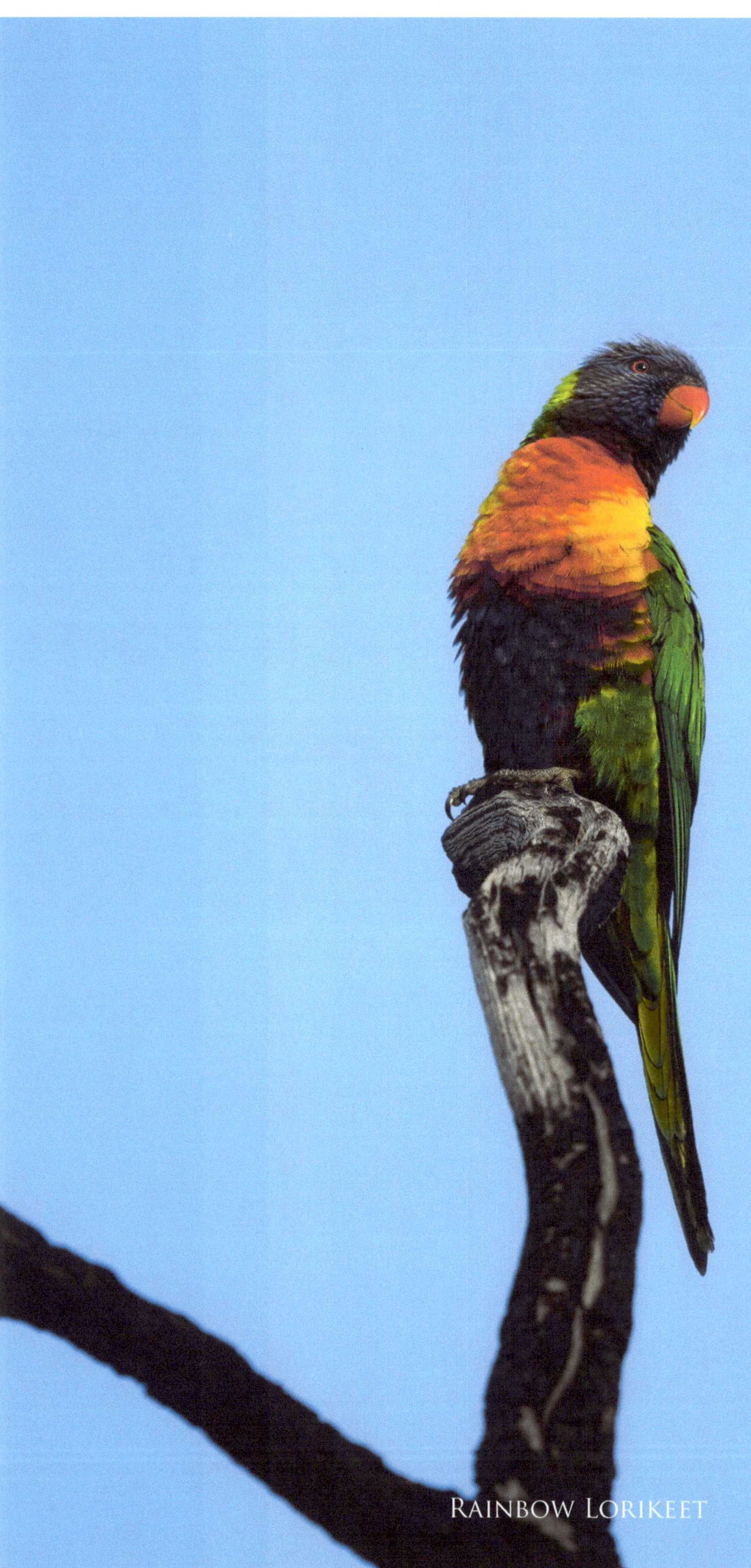

Rainbow Lorikeet

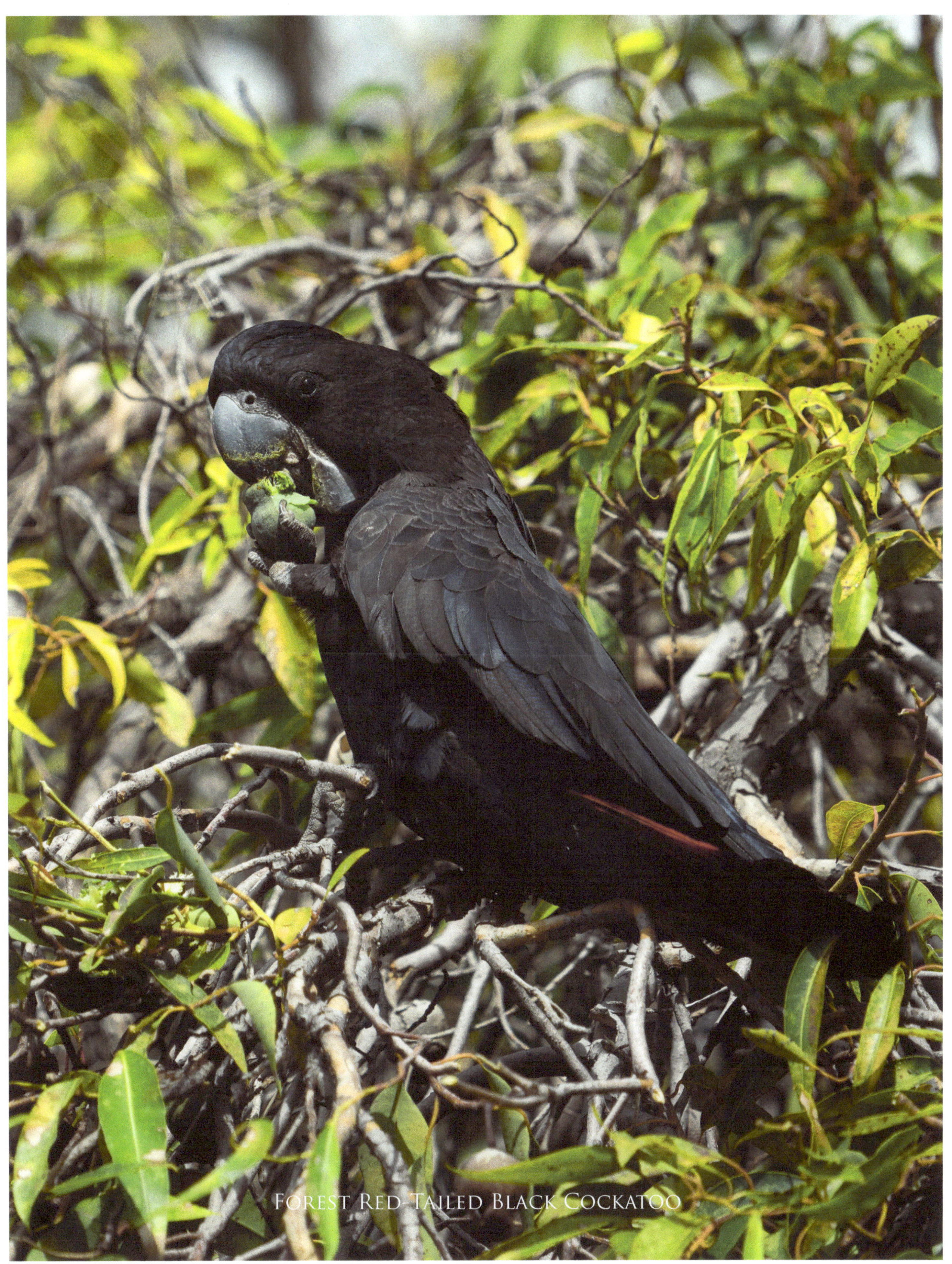

Forest Red-Tailed Black Cockatoo

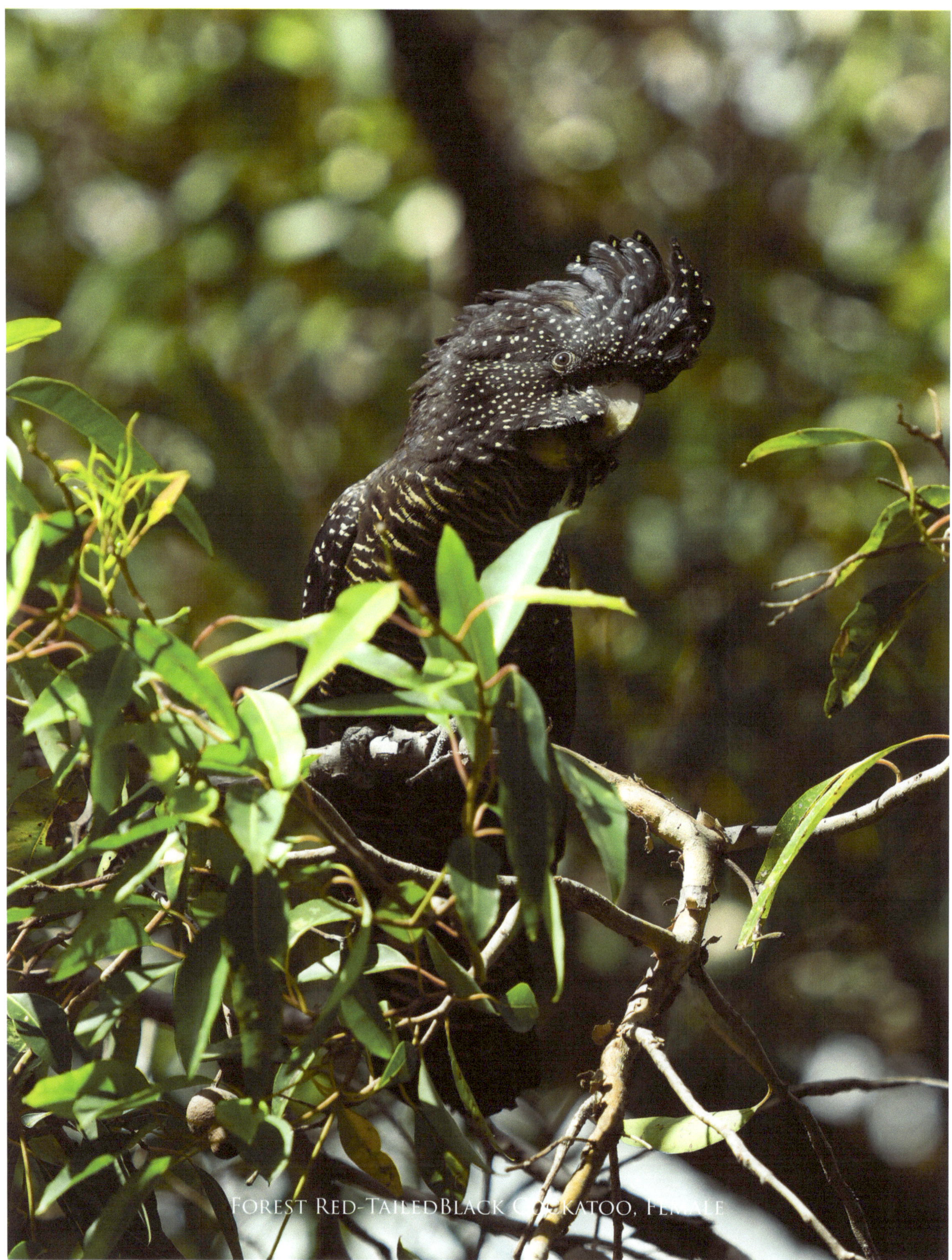

Forest Red-TailedBlack Cockatoo, Female

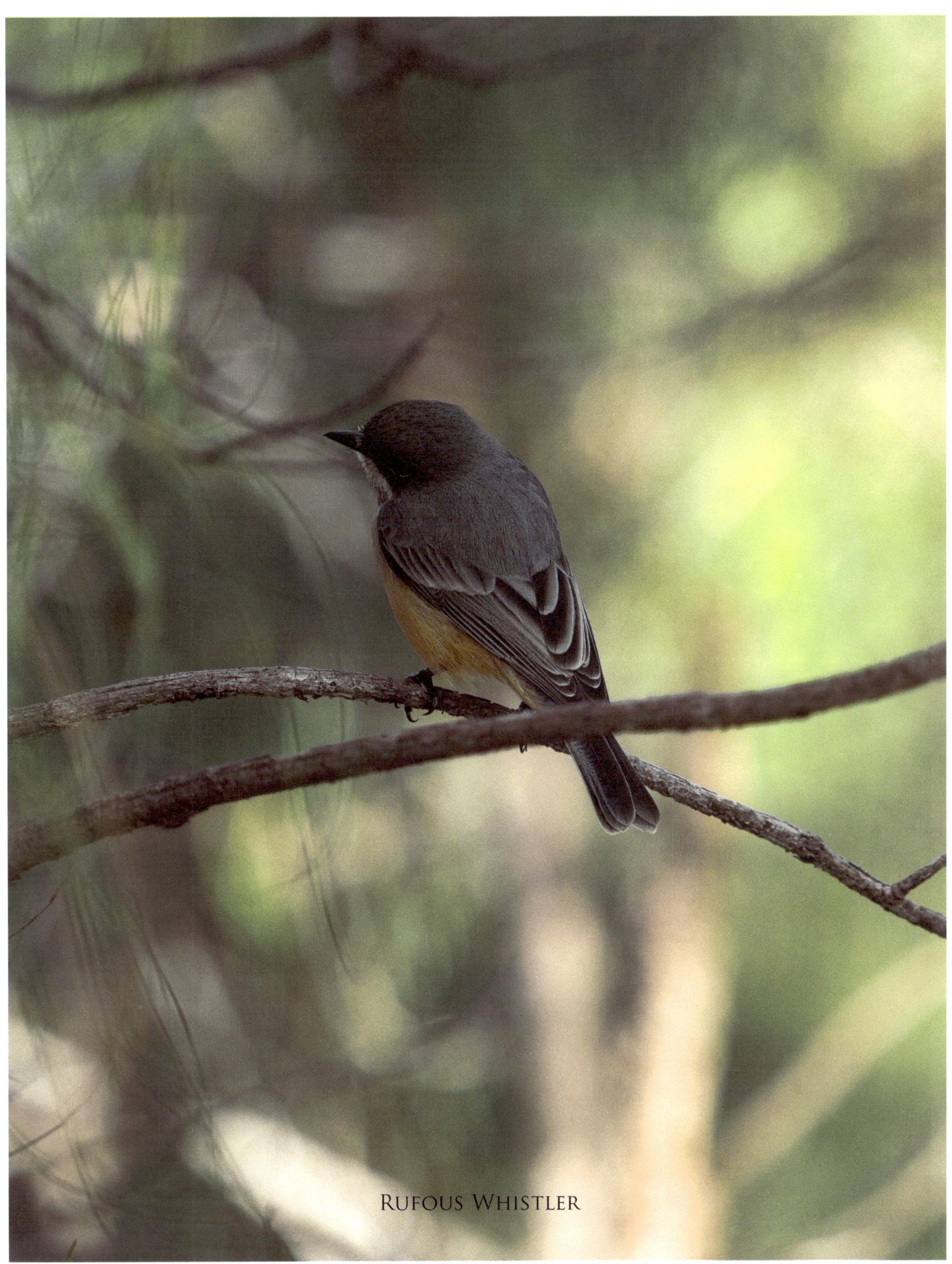

Rufous Whistler

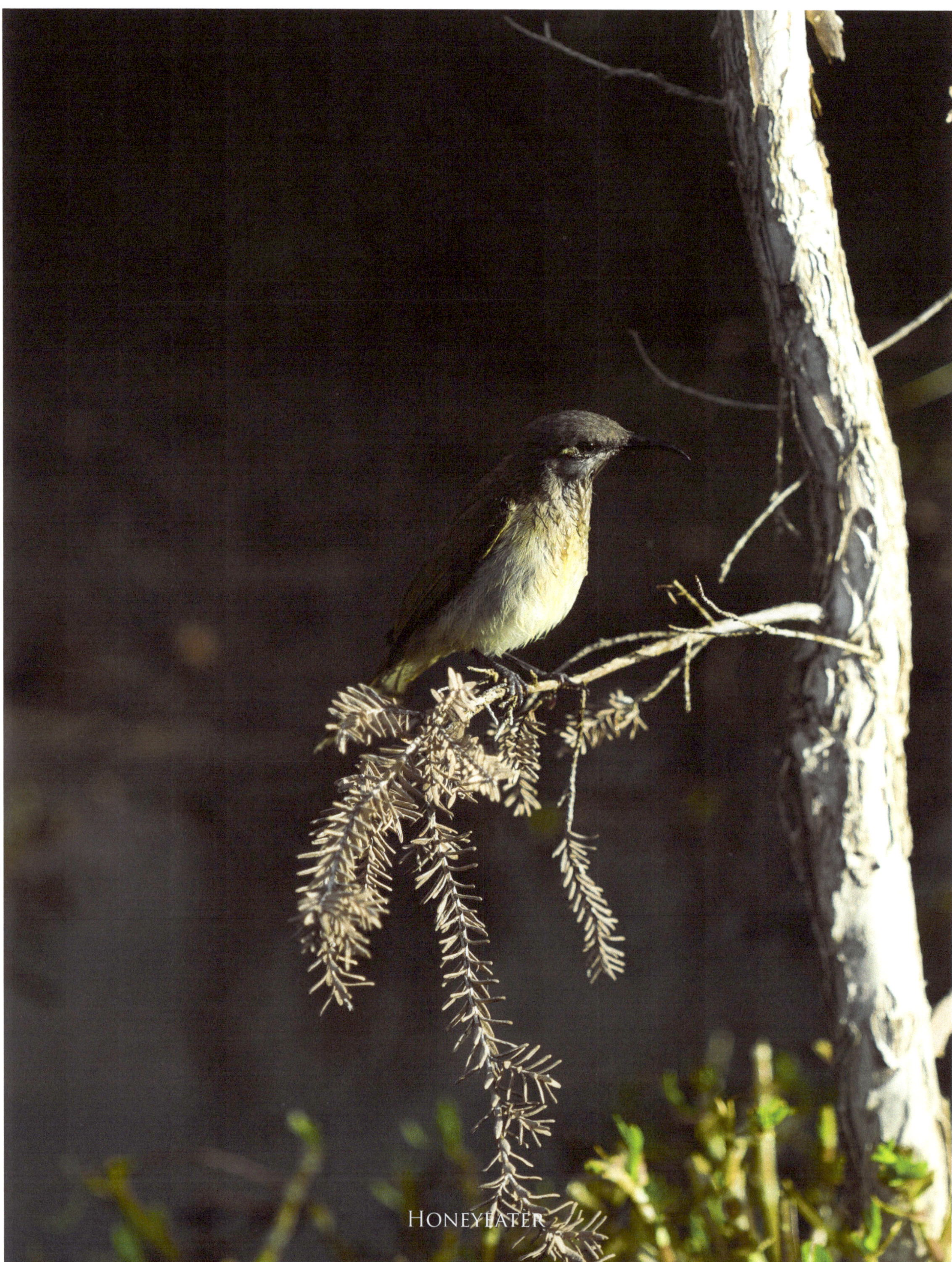

HONEYEATER

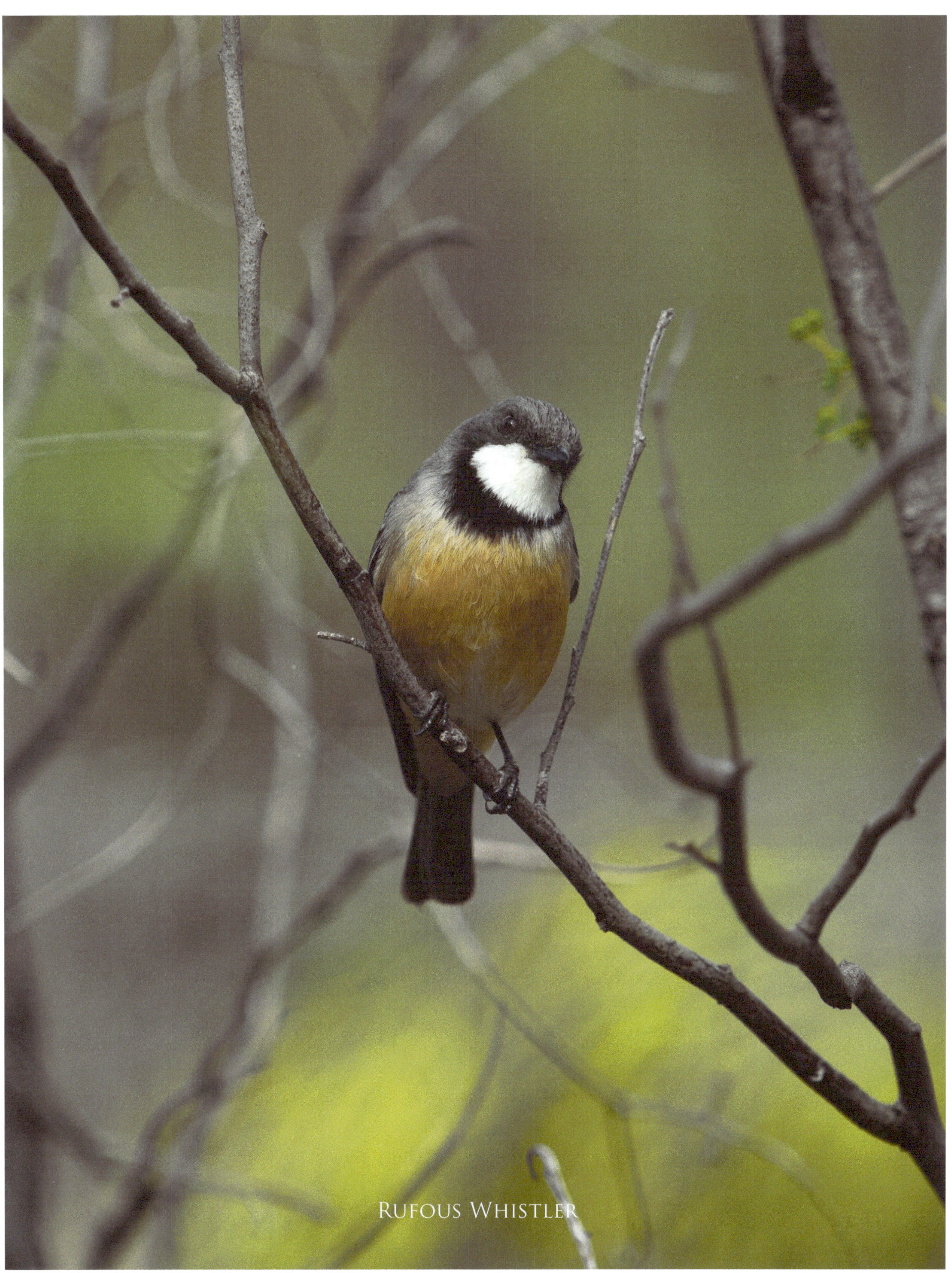

Rufous Whistler

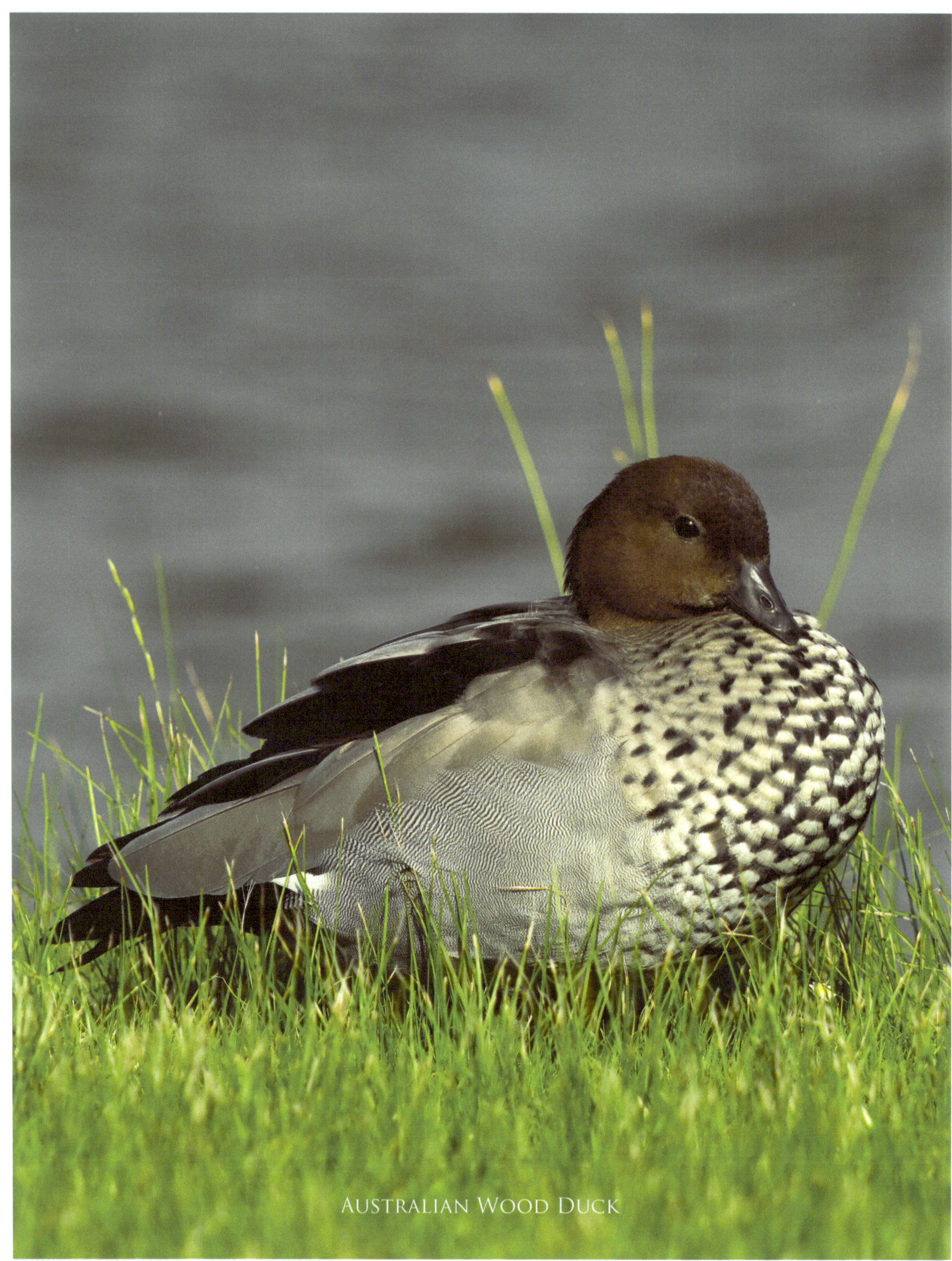

Australian Wood Duck

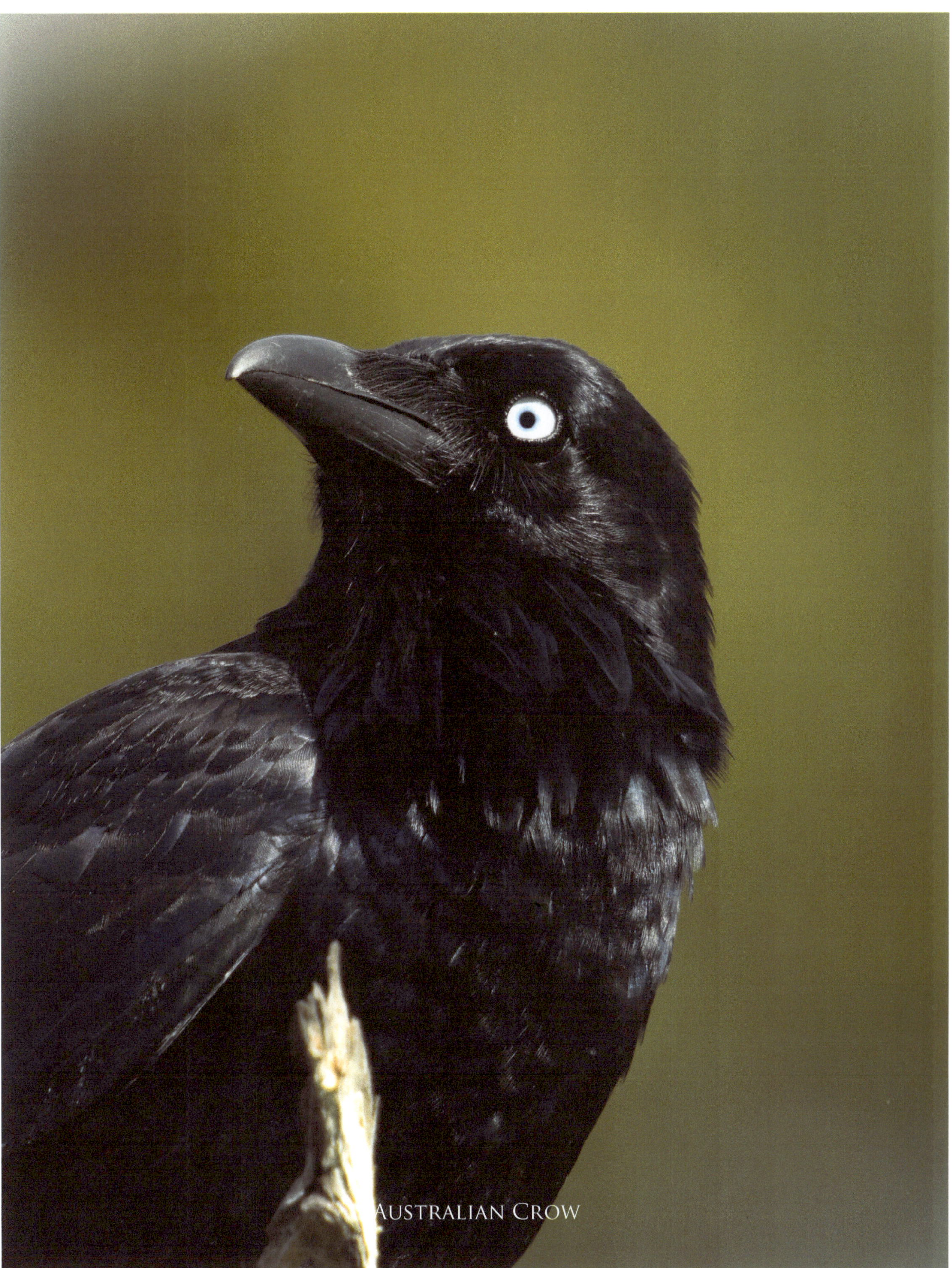

Australian Crow

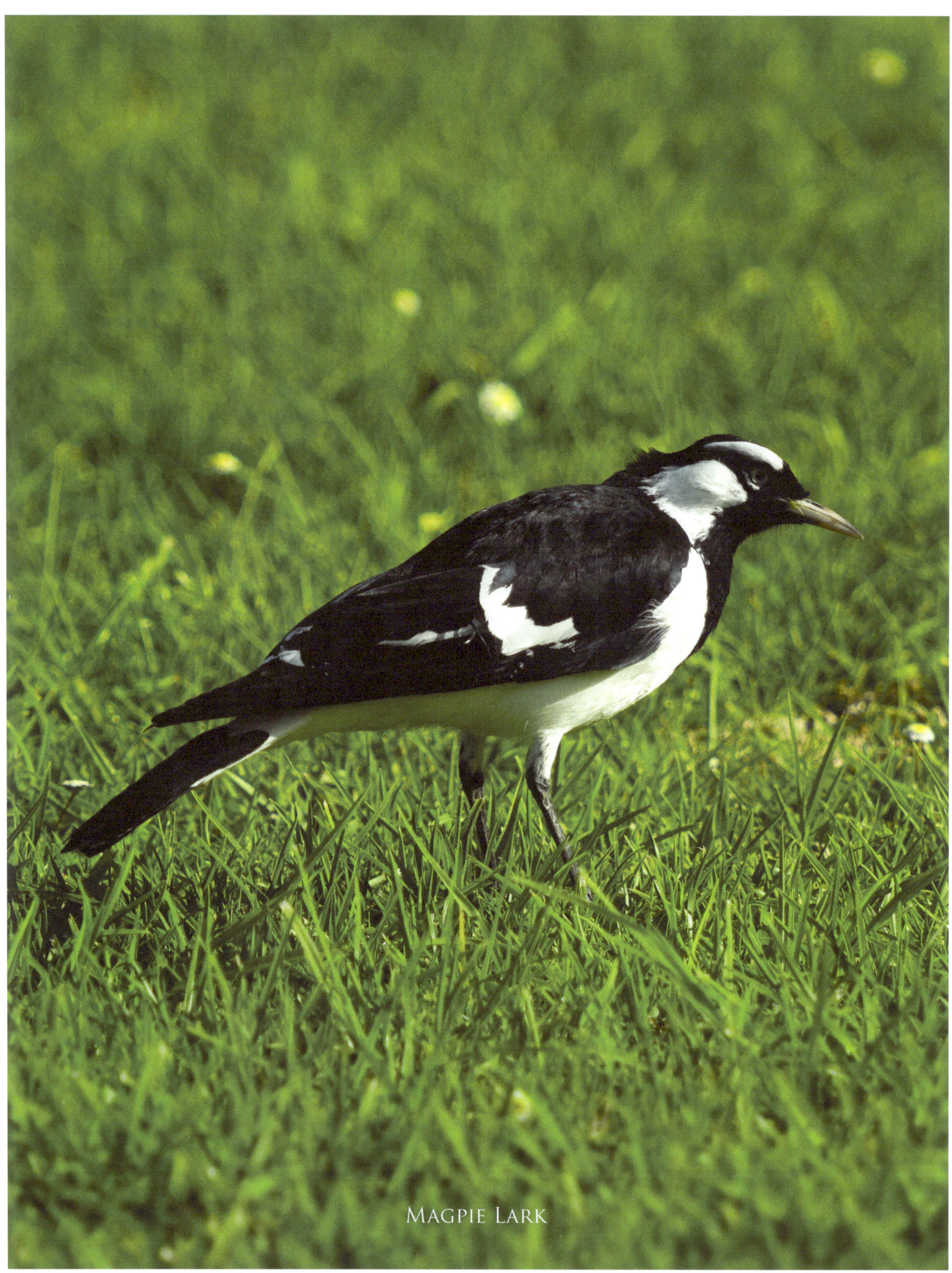

Magpie Lark

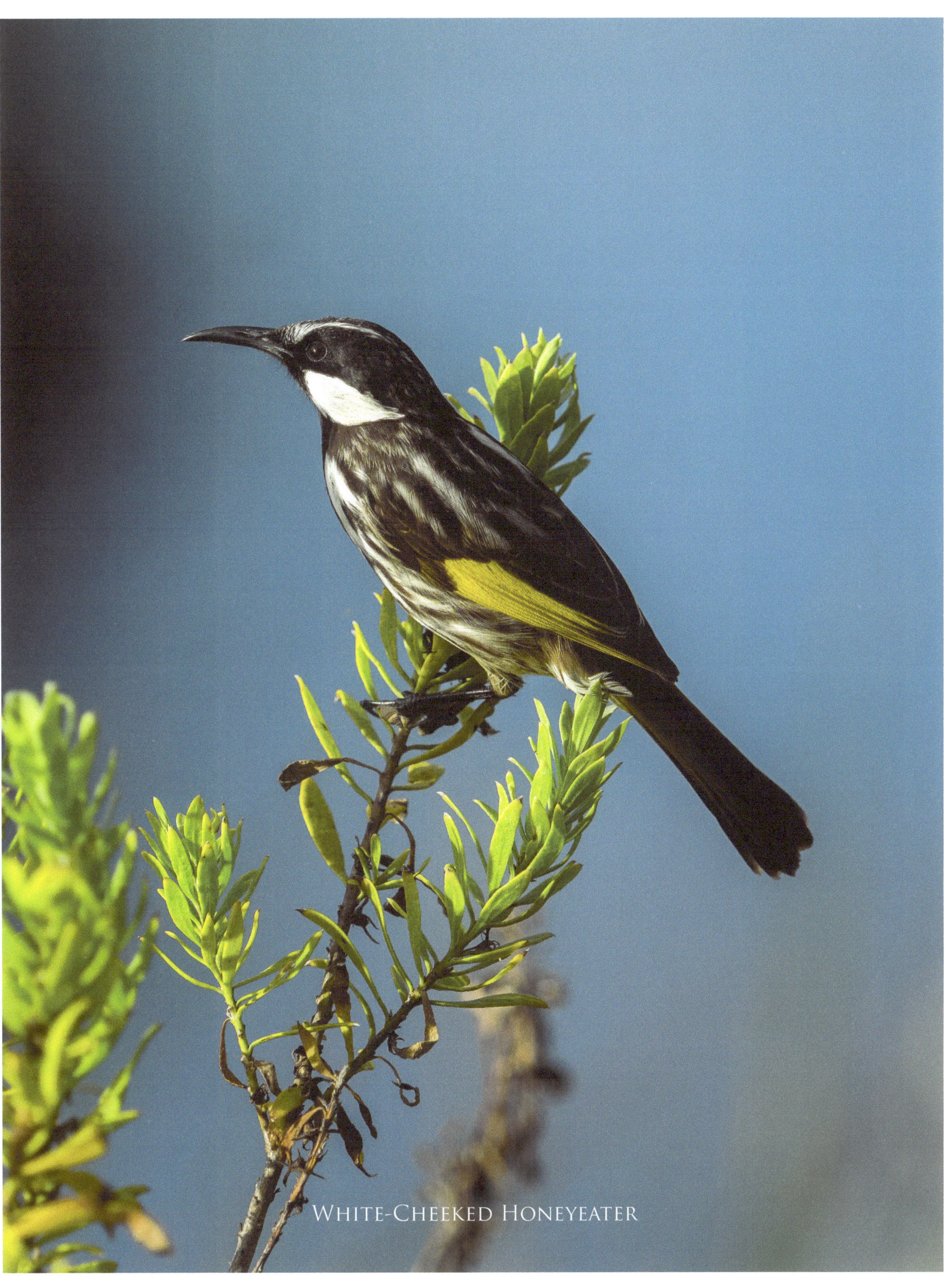

White-Cheeked Honeyeater

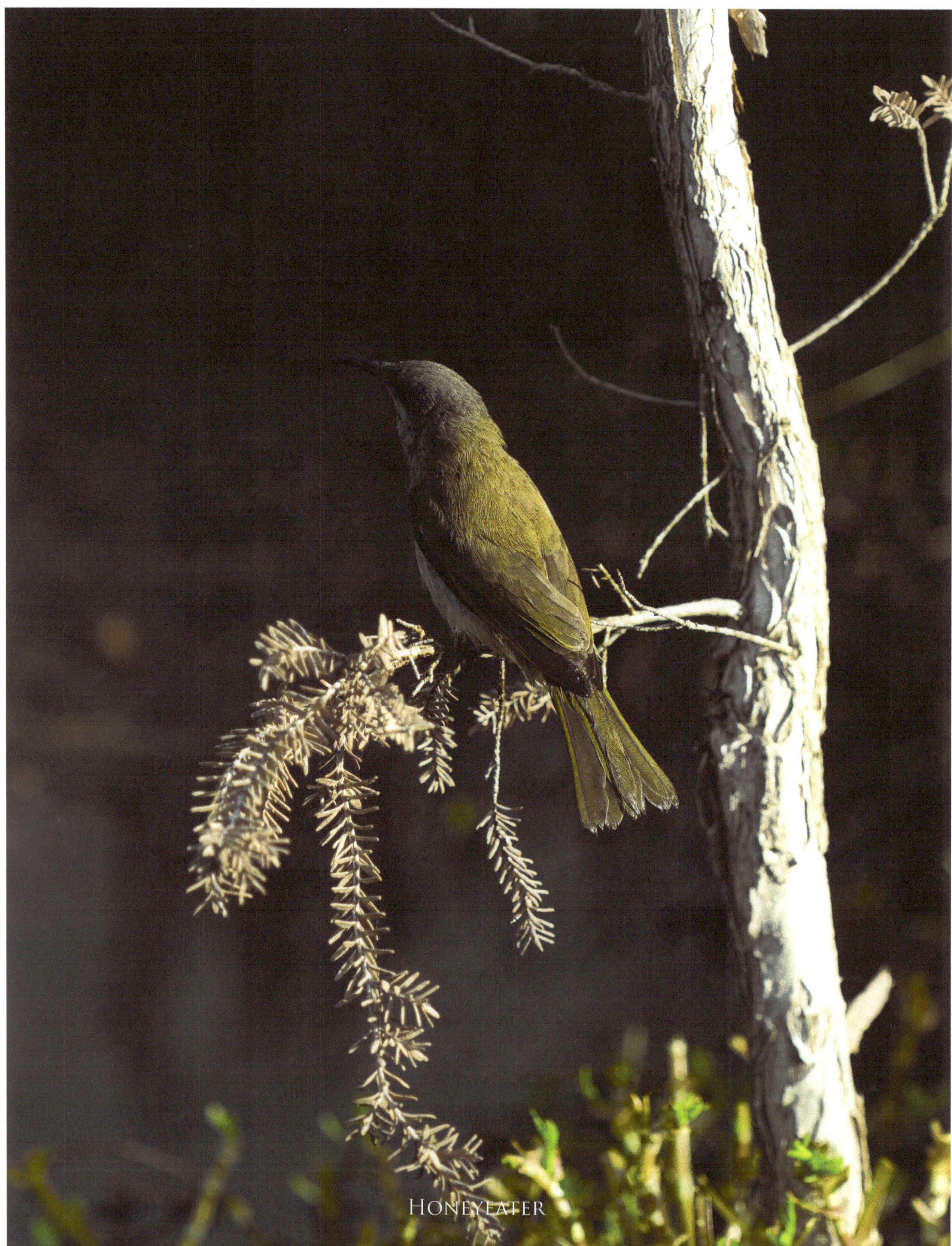

HONEYEATER

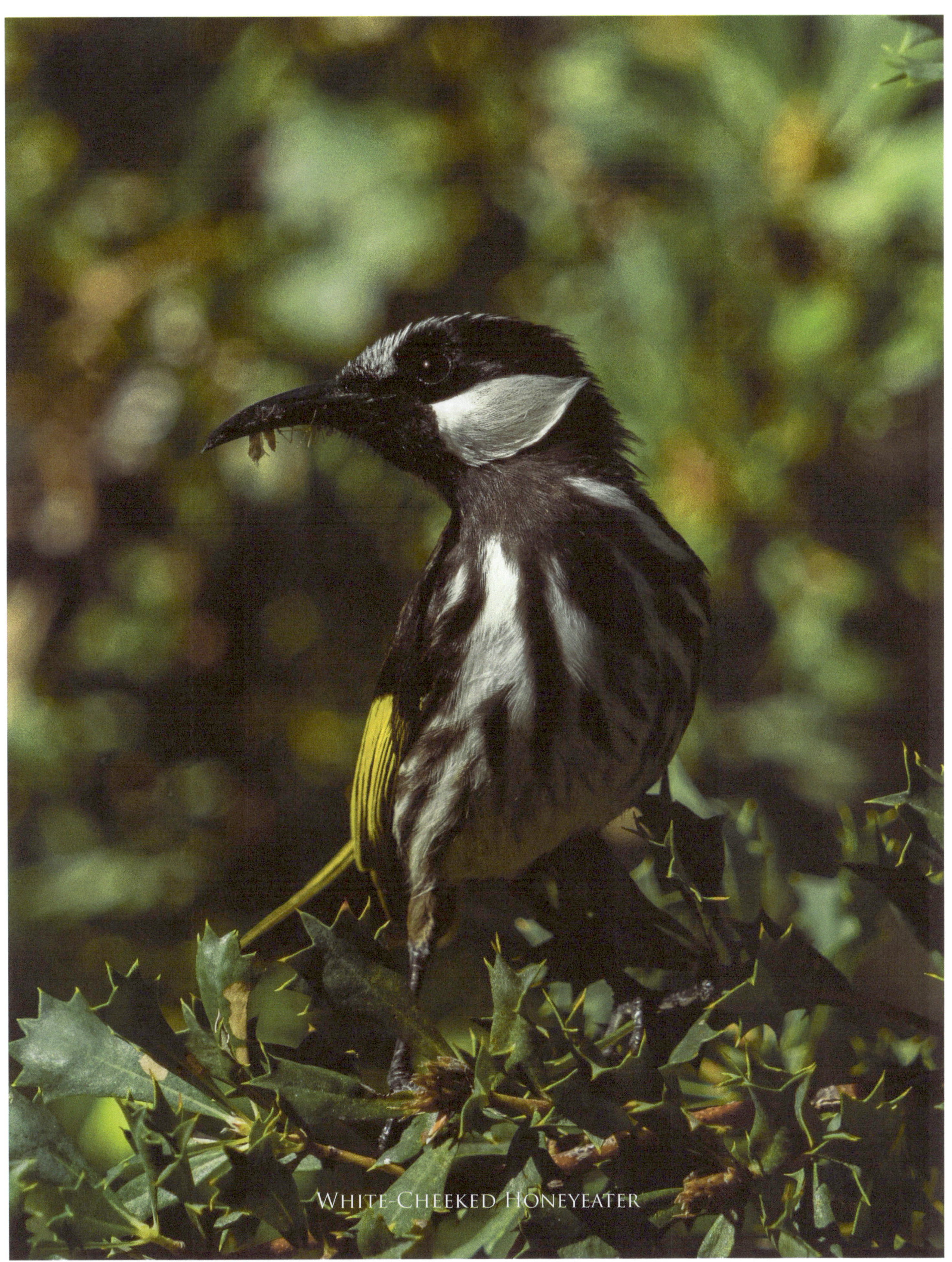

White-Cheeked Honeyeater

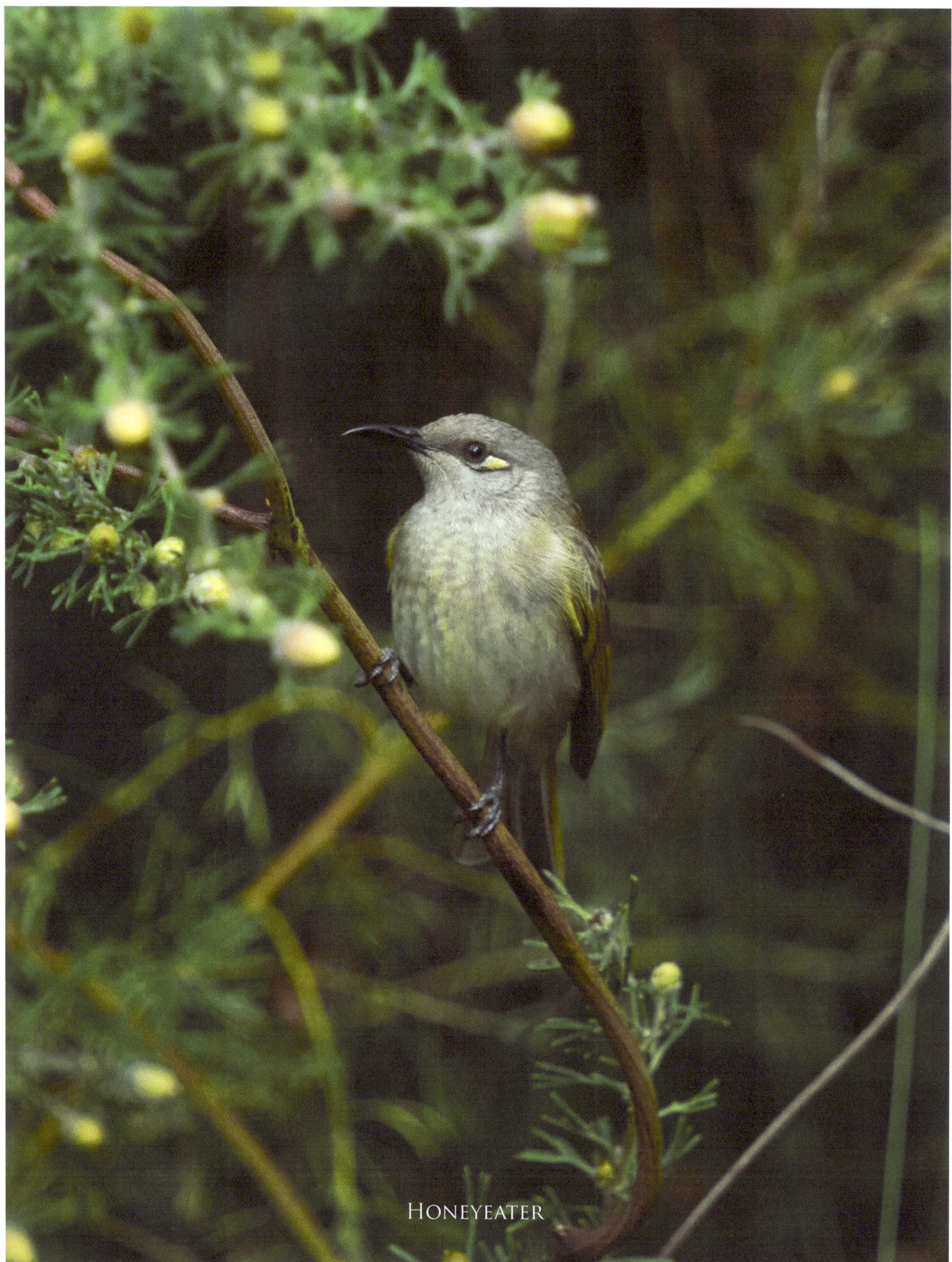

Honeyeater

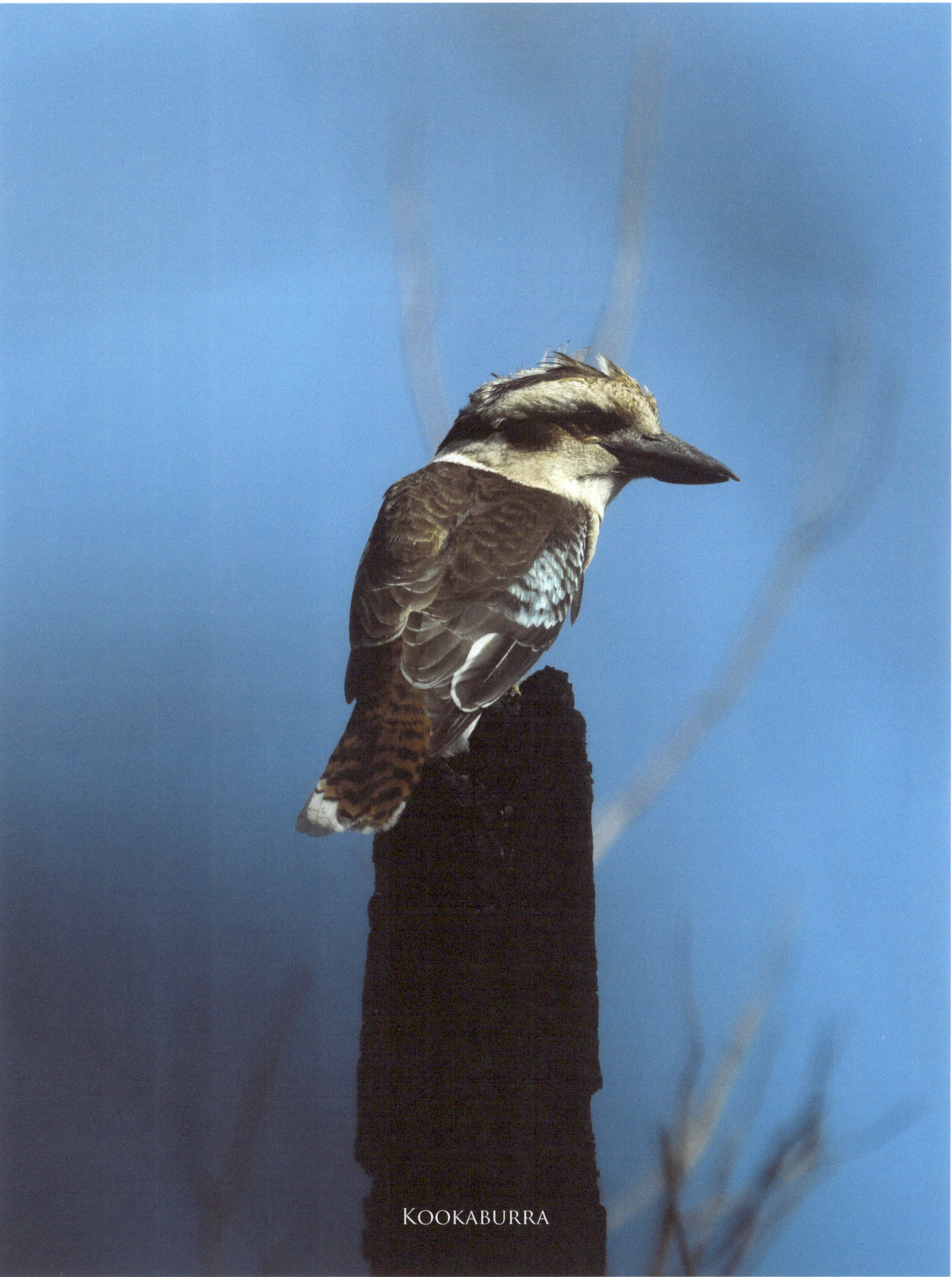

Kookaburra

www.ingramcontent.com/pod-product-compliance
Lightning Source LLC
LaVergne TN
LVHW071631100826
845154LV00007BA/130
9780998068237